THE BASICS OF

HOSHIN KANRI

THE BASICS OF

HOSHIN KANRI

Randy K. Kesterson

CRC Press
Taylor & Francis Group
Boca Raton   London   New York

CRC Press is an imprint of the
Taylor & Francis Group, an **informa** business

A PRODUCTIVITY PRESS BOOK

CRC Press
Taylor & Francis Group
6000 Broken Sound Parkway NW, Suite 300
Boca Raton, FL 33487-2742

Printed on acid-free paper
Version Date: 20140514

International Standard Book Number-13: 978-1-4822-1869-5 (Paperback)

Library of Congress Cataloging-in-Publication Data

Kesterson, Randy K.
    The Basics of Hoshi Kanri / Randy K. Kesterson.
        pages cm
    Summary: "The problem with most Hoshin Kanri books is they describe a methodology that is complex and overwhelming to most leaders and their companies. The need to essentially change the culture of the entire organization to make Hoshin work, just isn't practical for many companies when first starting out. Supplying clear explanations of the steps of hoshin kanri, this book advocates using Hoshin as an important tool to improve the existing planning and execution system while simultaneously working to move the culture of the organization forward"-- Provided by publisher.
    Includes bibliographical references and index.
    ISBN 978-1-4822-1869-5 (paperback)
    1. Business planning. 2. Organizational change. 3. Communication in management. I. Title.

HD30.28.K478 2015
658.4'01--dc23
        2014011560

Visit the Taylor & Francis Web site at
http://www.taylorandfrancis.com

and the CRC Press Web site at
http://www.crcpress.com

To my parents, Lyle and Barbara, for raising me

To my wife, Susan, for putting up with me

Contents

Preface

WHY I WROTE THIS BOOK

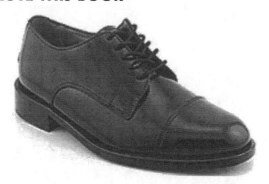

This is the story of a shoe that led to this book about Hoshin Kanri.

It was 2002 and I was flying home from Europe. It was a Friday, at the end of a long week of business travel. Between the bumps and lurches of the plane, I was working to put together a Strategy Formulation and Deployment approach for our company. My first attempt was pretty simplistic:

1. FORMULATE STRATEGY: Develop a differentiating strategy that results in a set of strategic objectives for the business.
2. DEPLOY THE STRATEGY: Carry out the strategy by cascading objectives down into the business units and functions, and by launching initiatives to attack the biggest problems, improve the key processes, and improve the overall business results.

We were using a few tools at that time:

TOOLS TO FORMULATE STRATEGY: A number of strategy formulation tools, including the Balanced Scorecard (along with some highly paid consultants)

TOOLS TO DEPLOY THE STRATEGY: The Balanced Scorecard, Lean Six Sigma, and Project Management

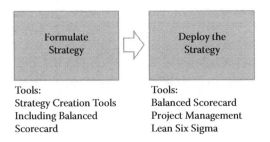

FIGURE P.1
Strategy Formulation and Deployment Approach: Version 1.0—A toolbox containing a few tools.

I remember sketching out our Current State. I will call what we were doing back in those days Version 1.0 of an evolving Strategy Formulation and Deployment Approach (Figure P.1). We had a toolbox with some tools. Period.

I was returning home from a trip to Switzerland where I had just met with the managing director of a company we had recently acquired. Gerhard and I had talked extensively (well, in retrospect, I talked a lot while he listened politely) about making significant changes within his business unit. I remember having the feeling as I was driving back to the airport in Zurich that the trip had been an utter failure. Gerhard was going to keep things the way they were before we had acquired them. I remember reflecting on how the resistance to change was incredible, especially at some of our newly acquired business units.

However, we couldn't give up. Gerhard's business unit's Return on Invested Capital (ROIC) was nowhere near our targeted level, and it was imperative that we (or I) fix this. Somewhere over the North Atlantic, after a couple of glasses of cabernet sauvignon, I remember drawing another diagram on the back of a napkin (literally), and this diagram consisted of a few more boxes. We will call this Version 1.1 (Figure P.2).

The process I drew consisted of four major steps, with Deploy the Strategy broken into three pieces:

1. FORMULATE STRATEGY: Develop a differentiating strategy that results in a set of strategic objectives for the business.
2. CASCADE THE STRATEGY: Flow the strategic initiatives (that came from the strategic objectives) down into the organization (via numerous scorecards).

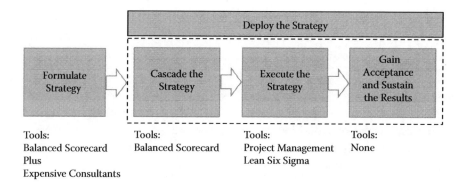

FIGURE P.2
Strategy Formulation and Deployment Approach: Version 1.1—With more details added on the deployment side.

3. EXECUTE THE STRATEGY: Attack the biggest problems, close the biggest gaps, improve key processes, and improve the overall business results.
4. GAIN ACCEPTANCE AND SUSTAIN THE RESULTS: Truly engage with the employees (engage with "their hearts and minds," as our Human Resources people would say) to eliminate resistance to the changes and improvements, and to sustain the hard-fought gains once they have been achieved.

I listed the tools we were using at that time in support of each of the four steps:

TOOL TO FORMULATE STRATEGY: Some strategy creation tools, including the Balanced Scorecard (along with some highly paid consultants)
TOOL TO CASCADE THE STRATEGY: The Balanced Scorecard
TOOLS TO EXECUTE THE STRATEGY: Lean Six Sigma and Project Management
TOOLS TO GAIN ACCEPTANCE AND SUSTAIN THE RESULTS: Nothing. Nada. Blank. We had no formal approach or a tool to help us in this area.

After I returned to the States, I sent our best Lean Six Sigma black belt, a guy I will call PhD Stan, to Switzerland to see what he could do about helping to make the required process-related changes happen within Gerhard's business unit.

Fast forward a couple of months. I recall looking up from my desk and seeing PhD Stan standing in my office doorway. Stan had his head down, and his body language indicated that he was thoroughly dejected. "They don't want to do it," he said. He went on to explain that he had used every analytical arrow in his analytical quiver, but he could not convince Gerhard, the managing director, and his team to make the necessary changes to improve their key business processes.

A few days later, I explained my problem to Martin, our vice president of Human Resources. After listening intently (as HR people tend to do), Martin suggested that what we needed was Organizational Change Management. OCM, he called it. I thanked him, but given its roots in the organizational development (OD) world, I assumed this OCM thing was grounded in a lot of hand-holding and singing of "Kum Ba Yah." It probably even included the use of the dreaded F-word, highly promoted by the HR/OD world—*feelings*.

However, I did some research and found that OCM was being employed successfully in industry. In fact, General Electric had been using an approach called the Change Acceleration Process (CAP) for several years with noteworthy results.

I remember thinking that we needed a similar approach—a methodology, model, toolset—that was synergistic with the Balanced Scorecard and the Lean Six Sigma tools; something we could use to eliminate the tremendous resistance to change we faced in Europe and in other parts of the business.

My conclusion at the time was that we were using the Balanced Scorecard to develop "balanced" top-level objectives, and we also were using it to some degree to deploy strategy by cascading the scorecards down into the organization. We also were using the Lean Six Sigma tools (in some areas, anyway) pretty successfully. However, the thing we lacked was a tool set, a methodology, an approach that could help us deal with resistance to change. We needed something that would work well with the Balanced Scorecard and Lean Six Sigma that we could deploy across the enterprise.

After doing quite a bit of research about OCM, I developed the diagram shown in Figure P.3.

I concluded that an OCM tool/approach/methodology was needed to help eliminate resistance to the major changes we were trying to make, i.e., to help gain acceptance/adoption, and to help us sustain the results.

I scheduled a meeting with my boss (Gerry) to talk about the plans for the proposed new Strategy Formulation and Deployment approach. I also

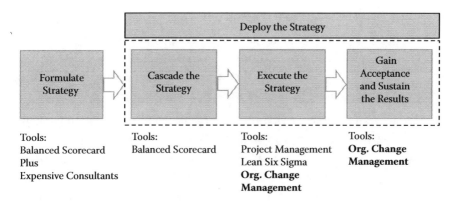

FIGURE P.3

Strategy Formulation and Deployment Approach: Version 2.0—A new tool is added (at least on paper).

invited a consultant who was working with us at the time, who happened to be my Lean Six Sigma black belt instructor from years earlier.

I explained the four-step model to my boss: (1) Strategy formulation, using some strategy creation tools including the Balanced Scorecard; (2) Cascading of the Strategy, using the Balanced Scorecard; (3) Strategy Execution, using the Lean Six Sigma tools and Project Management; and (4) Resistance Management, using an approach called Organizational Change Management. With that, Gerry held up his hand to indicate that I should stop talking. He said, "I have a change management approach that has served me very well for over 30 years in business." I can still see my consultant friend lean forward to listen more intently, as he has always been eager to learn about new, successful approaches. My boss then swung his foot up on the conference table, pointed to it, and said, "11-E" (his shoe size). "If they don't want to do it, I kick them in the ass," he said. Gerry called it his "11-E approach to change management." I will say that while my boss at the time had indeed perfected the art of 11-E, he was saying this mostly in jest. The meeting ended soon thereafter without a positive resolution (at least from my perspective).

I left that company shortly thereafter and was subject to the restrictions of a noncompete agreement that limited me from working for any company within an industry in which they competed. I knew I couldn't just sit at home and do nothing, so I decided to go into the world of management consulting, specializing in an area I wanted to learn more about. You guessed it—OCM.

Note: There are times when the 11-E approach is needed. A fire in the hallway doesn't call for consensus building. It calls for action. "The building is on fire, get the hell out of here!" And, there are also times and places for command and control management. For example, can you imagine a military environment without a command and control approach? But, when you are trying to drive strategy down into an organization, a command and control approach just doesn't work very well.

I knew from experience that the 11-E approach to change management was not entirely effective, so I went in search of a new, more enlightened approach. I intended only to remain in this field until my noncompete limitations expired, but I enjoyed it so much that I continued on that path for almost four years. The wealth of information that I learned in those four years about managing resistance and sustaining change proved extremely valuable. I consulted with a major bank during my time in change management consulting and I got some great first-hand exposure (positive and negative) to Hoshin Kanri. (Hoshin Kanri is a strategy deployment tool, approach, or system. It is an element of a larger management system introduced to the western world in the 1980s as Total Quality Management (TQM).) From that point on, I was hooked. I began studying the Hoshin approach and I talked to people, outside of the bank, who were using it with great success.

With the introduction of Hoshin Kanri, the result is a strategy deployment **system**, no longer just a box of tools (Figure P.4).

I continued to study Hoshin Kanri, reading every book and article I could find on the subject. I interviewed nearly 100 experts on the subject—practitioners, executives, consultants, professors, and authors; people who had experience with Hoshin, both good and bad. I also had the

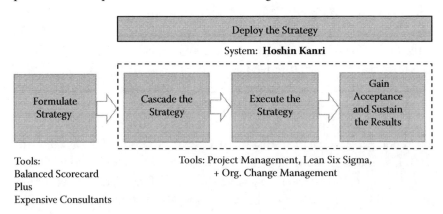

FIGURE P.4
Strategy Formulation and Deployment Approach: Version 3.0—A deployment system.

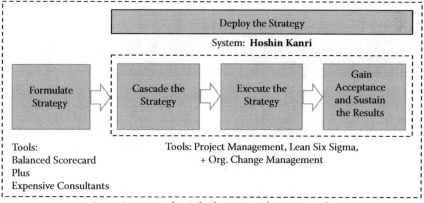

An Environment

FIGURE P.5

Strategy Formulation and Deployment Approach: Version 4.0—A supportive work environment.

opportunity to immerse myself inside Milliken & Company, a corporation with a very unique environment, one in which respect for the individual is paramount and safety is the primary value, not just an important metric.

What I learned from all of these experiences is that to gain maximum advantage, it is important to develop an overall work environment that allows Hoshin Kanri and the other strategy deployment and execution tools to thrive (Figure P.5).

A work environment is analogous to an onion, and most people spend their time working "on the surface" to deploy tools and employ new systems to improve processes. My conclusion is that to make extensive, sustainable gains within an organization, one must attack the issues found at "the core" of the "onion." One must change the "How," how the organization is led and managed (Figure P.6).

Lean Six Sigma, Project Management, and Organizational Change Management are all important sets of tools, and Hoshin Kanri is an important management system (Figure P.7).

This book is about Hoshin Kanri, but the writer has learned that Hoshin is but one piece of the puzzle in reshaping an organization.

Randy K. Kesterson

The names in this story have been changed, but the story is true.

FIGURE P.6
"The How" is at the core of the organizational "onion."

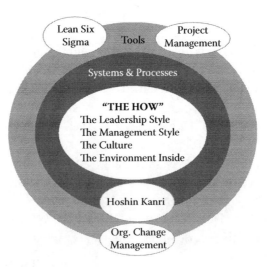

FIGURE P.7
Hoshin Kanri is a system that includes a set of tools.

Acknowledgments

I wish to personally thank the following people for their contributions to my inspiration and knowledge and other help in creating this book.

Thanks to Susan for her countless hours of expert editing, and to Chase for being so patient when I worked on the book instead of playing with him. Thanks to Mike, Nicole, Lori, Kris, Angela, and Jeffry D. for their unfailing moral support.

Thanks to David Thomas, Ellen Domb, Jane Dwyer, Lisa Boisvert, John Gaul, Kevin Grayson, Barry Witcher, Lois Gold, Tom Cluley, Gerhard Plenert, Paul Docherty, Tom Jackson, Bruce Sheridan, Jonathan Ngin, and James Hinkle for their help with the editing.

Thanks to the people who helped shape my career and my view of the world of work, to include Dudley Johnson, Larry Mitter, John Wood, George Yohrling, Blan Godfrey, Jeanenne LaMarsh, and Mike Mulligan.

Thanks to the Hoshin experts from all walks of life who were so generous with their time, allowing me to interview them, and/or obtain their comments for the book. Mini-Bios for these people can be found near the end of Chapter 3.

Thanks to the developers of Hoshin Kanri ... Dr. Deming, Dr. Juran, and the early adopters in Japan. And, thanks to the authors of the early Hoshin Kanri books written in English ...Bob King (1989), Yoji Akao (1991, with introduction by Greg Watson and translated by Glenn Mazur), Michele Bechtell (1993 and 1995), Bruce Sheridan (1993), Greg Watson (1994), Mora Minerva Melum and Casey Collett (1995), Michael Cowley and Ellen Domb (1997).

Introduction

I'm guessing that you are reading this introduction because you are looking for a simple explanation of Hoshin Kanri. I understand. When I started my Hoshin exploration, I was overwhelmed by the six-dimensional X-Matrices (only a slight exaggeration) and the "A3s for Every Occasion" found in some of the more advanced Hoshin Kanri materials.

I'm going to simplify it for you by explaining Hoshin Kanri through the telling of a short story. Chapter 1 of this book contains a story about a manufacturing executive, Jon Anderson. This story demonstrates how Jon uses a simple Hoshin Kanri approach to make significant change in his personal life. Chapter 2 of this book tells how Jon prepares to apply Hoshin Kanri to deploy strategy within his business. Chapter 3 of the book contains some fascinating excerpts from my real life interviews with some of the experts in the field of Hoshin Kanri.

Simplicity is the ultimate sophistication.

Leonardo da Vinci

Everything should be made as simple as possible, but not simpler.

Albert Einstein

Paraphrasing Leonardo da Vinci and Albert Einstein, I hope the book is simple enough for you, but not too simple.

1

The Basics of Hoshin Kanri: A Personal Example to Help Explain the Steps

If you do not change direction, you may end up where you are heading.

Lao Tzu

You have the brains in your head. You have feet in your shoes. You can steer yourself in any direction you choose. You're on your own, and you know what you know. And you are the guy who'll decide where to go.

Dr. Seuss

Discipline is the bridge between goals and accomplishment.

Jim Rohn

JON

I'd like to introduce you to Jon Anderson. Jon is a successful business man. He has enjoyed a career in manufacturing operations that propelled him quickly to the executive level he enjoys today. As a matter of fact, he has just accepted a new challenge with an aerospace company, IGC Aerospace, where sales are flat, and profit and cash flow are at unacceptable levels. Even with his expertise, he is finding the challenges of this environment overwhelming, topped with the stress of not seeing eye-to-eye with his boss.

Another stressor for Jon is the fact that his job requires frequent travel, taking him away from home and his family. He is happily married, but would like more one-on-one time with his wife, and his *teenage* kids.

"What are their names?" Seriously, he recognizes the distance growing between them and realizes that time is ticking away. He will soon wave goodbye as they leave for college just as he will wave goodbye to his chances to spend quality time with them.

Yes, all of the stress, all of the wishing things could be different. These grow right along with his waistline. How he longs for the days when he could run for miles with no aches and pains. At this point, he would be thrilled with a daily 30-minute walk. And, again, all that travel—airport food, airplane air, rushing to cocktail hours, dinners, endless meetings, jet lag—Jon knows something has to change.

Then, one day on a business trip, Jon struck up a conversation with an intriguing gentleman in the seat beside him on the plane. This man appeared to be in his midfifties, fit, and apparently successful, judging by his sport coat, shoes, and, especially, by the five-sided diamond charm Jon handed back to him after noticing he had dropped it on the floor. As a repayment of his kindness, the gentleman gave Jon a book. One that would change his life.

There was no publisher information or table of contents, only a simple title page, *The Little Book of Hoshin Kanri: A tool for changing your life.* The book started with an introduction explaining the term *Hoshin Kanri*.

INTRODUCTION TO *THE LITTLE BOOK*

The words *Hoshin* and *Kanri* have been translated to mean a number of things. A common definition in English is **strategy deployment**, and you often see a compass used as the image to represent the term. **Hoshin Kanri** is a strategic objective delivery system used in business. In this book, you will apply the basics of this process to make a significant personal change.

As you might imagine, it is much easier to deploy a strategy if you actually have one. So, before we get into the steps of Hoshin Kanri (i.e., strategy deployment), we are first going to use the Scan process to *create* your personal strategy for use in this exercise. Then, we will walk

Strategy Deployment: A process that follows Strategy Formulation. It uses the key objectives (e.g., the "Hoshins") that were developed in the Strategy Formulation process and makes them available for review and action throughout the organization, both vertically down through the organization's layers and across the organization's functions.

Hoshin Kanri: A strategy deployment tool, approach, or system. It is an element of a larger management system introduced to the western world in the 1980s as Total Quality Management (TQM).

through the Plan-Do-Check-Adjust (PDCA) cycle used in the Hoshin Kanri process, but, in this case, we will apply it to a personal objective.

Step 1: Scan (the Strategy Formulation process)
Step 2: Plan (the Hoshin Kanri process begins)
Step 3: Do
Step 4: Check
Step 5: Adjust

Step 1: Scan—Create a Vision and Assess Reality

This first step (Scan) is about **strategy formulation** and also identifying a few key objectives in support of the **strategy**.[1] This step starts with understanding where you are today and where you want to be a few years from now. You will create a personal vision for your future self, while keeping your feet firmly planted in today's reality.

The Scan Process

1. Develop your Personal Mission Statement
2. Define your Personal Values
3. Define your Personal Current State
4. Define your Personal Vision
5. Design your Personal Desired Future State
6. Identify the gaps between the Future and Current States
7. Prioritize the gaps; define your Personal Priorities

1: Develop Your Personal Mission Statement

It's important for a business to define its purpose, its reason for being in existence. In this case, it is important for you to take a few minutes to reflect on your personal mission (Figure 1.1). Consider your roles and your purpose in life.

Jon lists his roles and his purpose.

Total Quality Management (TQM) is a management system with a misleading name. The name is a misnomer because the system actually encompasses all elements of an organization, not just quality. TQM is considered to be an out-of-date term by some, but the author believes that the concepts remain valid to this day. This belief is supported by the fact that several organizations are employing TQM and Hoshin Kanri with great success as of the writing of this book.

Strategy Formulation: A process where strategy is created or revised.

Strategy: An overall approach to achieve what an organization proclaims in its purpose statements (Vision, Mission, Values), to include the determination of its strategic objectives. In this case, **Strategy** is an overall approach to achieve an individual's personal purpose and vision, to include the determination of his/her strategic objectives.

Mission: Why we are here. Why we exist. Our purpose. Our reason for being. In the personal Hoshin example, this includes the roles we play.

Define Your Mission:

Roles: Husband, father, executive, son, brother,
    uncle, community member, friend
Purpose: To fulfill all of my roles to the best of
    my ability

FIGURE 1.1
Your personal mission.

2: Define Your Personal Values

Values for an organization are the guiding principles that communicate the expected collective norms and behavior of everyone in the organization. In other words, values serve as the basis for making decisions within the organization and act as the foundation for communication with colleagues and customers. Your **personal values** are the guiding principles that serve as the basis for the decisions *you* make.

> **Personal Values:** Guiding principles that serve as the basis for the decisions you make.

Jon lists the teachings of his religion as his personal guiding principles.

3: Define Your Personal Current State

The next step for creating your strategy is to define your Personal Current State. Take a step back to consider your environment, your current life situation—your personal **Current State**, if you will. Let's start by examining your current Work-Life Balance (Figure 1.2).

> **Current State:** Our current reality.

The phrase *work-life balance* immediately conjures up the image of a simple weighing scale, with "work" on one side and "life" on the other. For most people, the weight on the "work" side easily tips the scale because "life" often is so far out of balance that it becomes a struggle between time

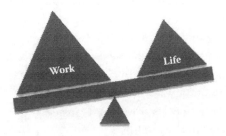

FIGURE 1.2
Work-Life Balance.

WORK	FAMILY
"ME" • My Body • My Mind • My Soul	Everyone & Everything Else

FIGURE 1.3
Your work-life balance.

spent at work and time spent with family or friends, or time spent pursuing personal interests. However, as tough as this is, it's even more complicated than this. As you will see, there are more than two facets to a well-balanced life (Figure 1.3).

There are at least four facets to a balanced life. These are time spent

- at work, earning a living;
- with immediate family;
- doing things for you, also known as "me time" or time for improving body, mind, and soul; and
- with everyone and everything else in the world.

Considering all of these facets, the image that comes to mind for some is a person trying to keep multiple dinner plates balanced and spinning in the air. It can certainly feel that way as life can be difficult to manage (and balance) at times.

Is your life currently in proper balance? And, in addition to the need to rebalance, are there also aspects of the facets of your life that you would like to change? If so, what changes do you want to make? The best place to start for identifying these changes is with an assessment of your current state.

Personal Current State Worksheet
List the things that describe your personal current state. Include both the favorable and unfavorable aspects of your current life situation. Think about where you are now in terms of your work and your immediate family. Think about your body, your mind, your soul. Think about everyone and everything else in your life, such as extended family, close friends, community, your education, your finances, etc. Where are you now with

YOUR PERSONAL CURRENT STATE	
INVOLVING WORK	**INVOLVING FAMILY**
I like my new job so far Traveling too much 4+ days a week 3 to 4 weeks per month In office from 7 am until 6 pm+ Work every Saturday	Strong marriage But, no "date nights" with Cathy Kids don't know me anymore And, I don't know them
ABOUT "ME" (Involving my body, my mind, and my soul)	**Involving Anyone or Anything Else in the World**

30 lbs. overweight
Total cholesterol at 280+
No time for exercise
Eating too much fat and sugar
No time for reading (for fun)
Never go to church with my family
	No time for golf
	No poker nights with buddies
	No time for snow skiing
	No extended family time:
	   Parents live 1,000 miles away
	   Rarely see siblings and their kids
	   Rarely see old friends from school

FIGURE 1.4
Your Personal Current State.

each of these things? What is your Personal Current State? Quantify where you can.

Jon contemplates these questions deeply, then enters his responses into the current state diagram. Where possible, he includes a "measure" to help explain his current situation (Figure 1.4).

4: Define Your Personal Vision

For an organization, vision is the picture of the future, i.e., where the business is going. Your **personal vision** is your dream for the future. It's your picture of the future for you.

Personal Vision: Your dream for the future. It's your "picture" of the future for you.

After considering his dream for his personal future, Jon enters the following in the little book.

Define Your Personal Vision
To be the best I can be in my various life roles. Healthy, helpful, happy, and successful.

5: Your Desired Future State

As you head toward your personal vision, your **desired future state** is your expectation for where you should be at a specific point in time.

For this exercise, pick a specific point in time, say, a few years from now. Think about what you like about your Personal Current State diagram and what you dislike about it. Now, bring the favorable things forward into your Future State diagram; the things you want to retain as you move forward with changes in your life.

> **Desired Future State:** As we head toward our Vision, this is our expectation for where we should be at a specific point in time. For example, three years from today.

Consider again each facet of the diagram. Ask yourself, "Where do I want to be a few years from now in terms of work and immediate family?" Think about your body, your mind, your soul. Then, once again, think about everyone and everything else in your life. Where do you *want to be* with all of these things? What is your Personal Desired Future State? Once again, try to quantify or think about how you will measure these things. For example, if your Desired Future State is that you want to improve your health, a measure may be in eating more fruits and vegetables or exercising three days a week or having annual checkups.

Jon contemplates his future and decides to define his desired future state at a point three years from now. He enters his responses into the boxes. Again, he attempts to include a measure or a metric to explain his desired future situation (Figure 1.5).

6: Identify the Gaps

Take some time to compare your personal Current State and your personal Desired Future State. Now, identify the "gaps." A **gap** is a difference between the Current State and the Future State, i.e., things that will require change. If you have a lot of gaps, consider which ones are the most significant. What are the biggest, most important gaps that separate your personal reality from your vision?

> **Gaps:** The difference between the Current State and the Future State. Things that will require change.

The diagram (Figure 1.6) shows how a transition is needed to move you from your current state, i.e., from today's reality, to your desired future state, heading toward your personal vision.

Jon studies his Personal Current State and Desired Future State diagrams and enters a few items into the "Identifying the Gaps" Worksheet (Figure 1.7).

YOUR PERSONAL DESIRED FUTURE STATE **Your Personal Vision** **As of date: 3 Years from Today**	

INVOLVING WORK
 	
Less overnight business travel!
No more than 4 nights away from home
  per month
Leave office by 5:45 pm!!!
Only work 2 Saturdays a month, and
  when I do, home before noon
	INVOLVING FAMILY
	
	More "date nights" with Cathy
	
	More quality time with kids
	  Get to know them again!

ABOUT "ME" (Involving my body, **my mind, and my soul)** Weight reduced by 30 lbs. (and maintained for a year) Total cholesterol <200 Exercise! (5 days a week) Eat better (diet plan TBD) Read 1 book a month (for pleasure) Go to church 3 times a month	**Involving Anyone or Anything Else** **in the World** Time for golf and snow skiing Poker nights with buddies See parents 2 times a year See siblings 2 times a year See old friends from school every year

FIGURE 1.5
Your Personal Desired Future State.

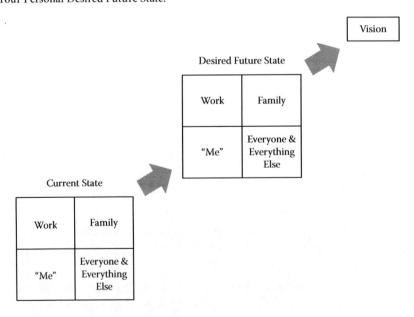

FIGURE 1.6
The change: From Current State to Desired Future State, toward your Vision.

Identifying the Gaps Worksheet

List your biggest gaps, in no particular order:

My weight: lose weight and keep it off!

My total cholesterol level!

Less time at work

Fewer nights spent away from home on business travel

More quality time spent with Cathy and the kids

More church attendance

More time for golf

More snow skiing. Maybe twice a year?

More reading for pleasure

More time with friends—new friends nearby and old friends far away

More time with extended family (parents, brother, sister, etc.)

More poker night events with my buddies

FIGURE 1.7
Identifying the Gaps Worksheet.

7: Your Personal Priorities

Now that you have defined your gaps, it's time to prioritize them. You can't change everything at once, so you need to decide where you will focus your attention for the next 12 months. Three tools/approaches will be used to help you: something called "Catchball," Stephen Covey's "Urgent versus Important" matrix; and the Interrelationship Digraph (a.k.a., the ID).

Catchball

So far, the Personal Hoshin process has involved only you. Now, it's time to engage others in the process. One tool used in Hoshin Kanri for getting constituents involved and engaged in discussing business objectives is **Catchball**. In the book, *Introduction to Hoshin Kanri: Policy Deployment for Successful TQM*,[2] Greg Watson describes it this way:

> **Catchball:** An interactive process of tossing items and possibilities back and forth like a game of "catch." It sometimes results in changes to proposed objectives, means, and measures.

> An analogy for this approach—which the Japanese call Catchball—is that people participate in a dialog in much the same way as a circle of young children play catch with a baseball. We sometimes call this technique "tossing an idea around."

What constituents should you involve in your personal Catchball process? Loved ones, very good friends, trusted advisors—anyone you feel

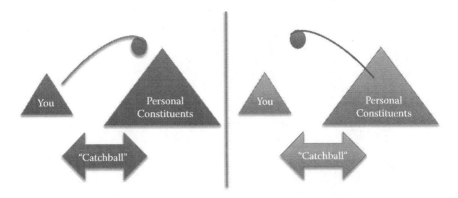

FIGURE 1.8
The Catchball Process: Steps 1 and 2.

comfortable having involved, but ideally also **committed to** your personal change plan (Figure 1.8).

Jon chuckled as he recalled the story of the bacon and egg breakfast.

> **Question**: *In a bacon and egg breakfast, what's the difference between the chicken and the pig?*
> **Answer**: *The chicken is involved, but the pig is committed!*

He decides to engage Cathy and the kids as his own personal constituents in his personal change plan. He initiates a Catchball session. Jon shares his list of 12 gaps. Suffering through some ridicule and eye rolling, he explains that Catchball involves tossing some ideas around—his ideas to them and then their ideas, thoughts, and honest feedback back to him. The result is a refined and, hopefully, an improved plan. One they all partially own and can buy into.

Jon suggests using Covey's "First Things First" approach to prioritize his list as they give their feedback. In this approach, Covey suggests prioritizing things based on where they fall in a simple "important/urgent" matrix. "Important but Not Urgent" items are probably the best candidates for priority items. The "Important and Urgent" items (e.g., fixing a leaky faucet) are more likely "Just Do It" items, not in need of an implementation plan.

Figure 1.9 includes some examples. For instance, a crying baby is "Important and Urgent," and some phone calls fall into the same category, while planning and exercise might not be considered urgent, but they can be very important over the longer term.

	Urgent	Not Urgent
Important	Crying baby Kitchen fire Some calls	Exercise Vocation Planning
Not Important	Interruptions Distractions Other calls	Trivia Busy work Time wasters

FIGURE 1.9
Covey's "First Things First" matrix. (Covey, S. R., A. R. Merrill, and R. R. Merrill. 1994. *First Things First*. New York: FIRESIDE. With permission.)

	Urgent	Not Urgent
Important	Some work issues	Diet and exercise Family Church Friends
Not Important		Reading Golf Poker nights Snow skiing

FIGURE 1.10
Jon's "First Things First" Matrix.

Jon and family discuss where each of his gaps should fall on Covey's matrix. A lot of discussion and polite arguing ensues (Figure 1.10).

By using the Important/Urgent matrix, they eventually narrow his list to eight top priorities (Figure 1.11), *eliminating four items from his original list.*

Jon also uses this as an opportunity to ask Cathy and the kids for their ideas on fun things to do to spend more time together. By giving his family an opportunity to offer ideas, he also gains their commitment and support for meeting these objectives. His son comments that it's been a long time since they played basketball together. Cathy suggests more three-mile walks. And his daughter wisely points out that taking on so many difficult objectives seems a bit overwhelming. Together, they use a tool called an

---

Jon's "Top 8" Priorities

My weight: lose weight and keep it off!

My total cholesterol level!

Less time at work

Fewer nights spent away from home on business travel

More quality time spent with Cathy and the kids

More church attendance

~~More time for golf~~

~~More snow skiing. Maybe twice a year?~~

More reading for pleasure

~~More time with friends—new friends nearby and old friends far away~~

More time with extended family (parents, brother, sister, etc.)

~~More poker night events with my buddies~~

FIGURE 1.11
Jon's "Top 8" priorities.

Interrelationship Digraph (ID) (Figure 1.12), *a cause and effect diagram that helps to prioritize items and identify **drivers** and outcomes. The drivers become candidates for Jon's personal Hoshins.*

   The Drivers:
     C: Less time at work
     F: Less overnight travel
     D: Exercise more
     E: Eat better

Note: Much more about the Interrelationship Digraph can be found in Appendix B.

From the Covey matrix and the Interrelationship Digraph (ID) exercise, Jon and his family decide on his two top personal priorities for the next 12 months (Figure 1.13).

You have defined your top personal priorities for the year. Next, you will turn them into **Objectives**. Make sure to keep the S.M.A.R.T. criteria in mind when defining your objectives.

Interrelationship Digraph (ID): Sometimes called the Root Cause tool because it helps identify the hidden causes. It shows the cause and effect relationships and helps to analyze the links between different aspects of a complex situation.

Driver: The elements in an Interrelationship Digraph with the most outgoing arrows are causes. They also might be root causes.

Objectives: This is the "what" we are working to achieve. It's most likely an element of our Desired Future State. This is a source of confusion because some use Goals, others use Objectives, some define a hierarchy where a Goal is superior to an Objective or vice versa. Within this book, we will simply say *Objectives*.

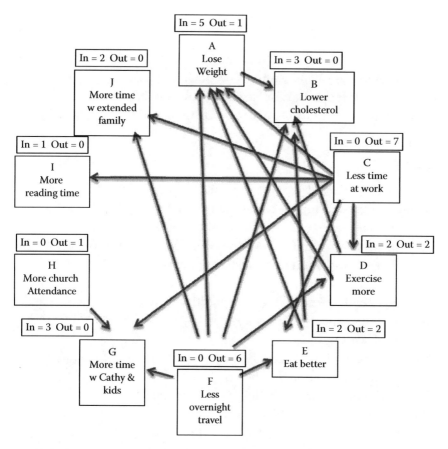

FIGURE 1.12
Interrelationship Digraph.

Top Priorities for Next 12 Months

- Lose weight (and keep it off)
- Improve family/work life balance

FIGURE 1.13
Jon's "Top 2" priorities.

Specific: Explain *what* in clear terms
Measureable: Quantify or at least suggest an indicator of progress
Assignable: Specify *who* will do it
Realistic: Within a practical range of achievement
Time-related: Specify *when* the result(s) can be achieved

Jon and family apply the S.M.A.R.T. criteria and develop two objectives:

Objective (Hoshin) #1: Achieve and maintain a healthy weight
Measures: Lose 30 lbs within 20 weeks from today
Objective (Hoshin) #2: Improve My Family/Work Balance
Measures: 60± hours of quality family time per month

Step 2: Plan

Great work in Step 1. You have identified your desired personal future state and your critical few objectives for the next 12 months; in other words, your personal **Hoshins**. Now, you will create your **plan** to get there. You have defined *what* you intend to accomplish, now, you need to describe *how* you intend to accomplish each objective. You also need to define the **Means** for each objective and the **Measures**.

Jon's plan contains two Hoshins and each has a way to measure it. Each Hoshin has one or more Means; in other words, the How to achieve the What. Each Means has a Measure and also a specific due date. You will note that he omitted the Who from the planning worksheets given that every Who was Jon.

Hoshins: The critical few or the BIG, "breakthrough" objectives.

Plan: Recognize an opportunity and plan a change.

Means: This is the "how;" how the objectives (or Hoshins) will be attained. Many names are used for this, e.g., Strategies, Tactics, Actions, Initiatives, etc.

Measures: These are the metrics that help us assess our progress toward our Desired Future State or our Objectives.

Planning Worksheet

Objective (Hoshin) #1 (Figure 1.14)*:* Achieve and maintain a healthy weight
Measures: Lose 30 lbs within 20 weeks from today
Objective (Hoshin) #2 (Figure 1.15)*:* Improve My Family/Work Balance
Measure: 60± hours of quality family time per month

Bowling Chart

The next step in Hoshin typically involves developing a **Bowling Chart**. This tool's name evolved because it resembles the scorecard for the game of bowling, which includes 12 frames, similar to the

Bowling Chart: Named after the scorecard used in the game of bowling, it's a visual management tool used in conjunction with improvement projects.

The Means (HOW)	Measures	WHEN/WHO
1. Use a personal trainer or health mentor	Identify trainers Select trainer Start program	By Tuesday By Friday Next Monday
2. Find and follow a healthy diet	Talk to Dr. Garcia Compare options Start Program	This Wednesday By Friday Saturday
3. Work out during lunch on weekdays. Walk with Cathy in evenings and on weekends.	Get gym bag for change of clothes Get new walking shoes Put bike rack on car Walk or bike during lunch four days a week 30-minute walk with Cathy, five times a week	Today Today Today Begin tomorrow Begin this evening

FIGURE 1.14
Plan for change #1.

The Means (HOW)	Measures	WHEN/WHO
1. Leave work at a reasonable time	By 5:30 pm, four nights a week	Beginning Monday
2. Limit Saturday work at the office	No more than (2) Saturdays per month, home before noon	Begin next weekend
3. Limit business travel nights away from home	Four nights per month max	This month
4. When at home, BE at home; spend quality time with wife and kids	Kids: 1+ hour per night on weekdays and 2+ dedicated hours per day on Saturday & Sunday	Starting today
	Cathy: One dinner date each month and one lunch date each week (and time walking together at least five times a week)	Starting today

FIGURE 1.15
Plan for change #2.

	Month	1	2	3	4	5	6	7	8	9	10	11	12
Weight Loss Cumulative	Target in lbs.	−2	−6	−14	−22	−30	−30	−30	−30	−30	−30	−30	−30
	Actual												
Quality Family Time	Target in hrs.	30	60	60	60	60	60	60	60	60	60	60	60
	Actual												

FIGURE 1.16
Jon's Bowling Chart.

12-month annual planning period. What is it for? A Bowling Chart is used in business to "keep score." It's an excellent visual management tool for any type of improvement project. You can think of it as a time-phased to-do list.

In the worksheet in Figure 1.16, enter your personal Hoshins and the measure you will use to track your progress.

Jon develops his personal Bowling Chart to track his weight loss and the time spent with his family. His plan involves losing 2 lbs. in month 1, 4 lbs. in month 2, 8 lbs. in months 3, 4, and 5, for a cumulative total of 30 lbs. by the time Jon starts month 6.

Jon's plan for family time involves spending 60 hours a month of "quality time" with his family, starting with 30 hours in month 1 to allow him (and them) some time to "ease into" the change. He decides to use "voice of the customer" from his wife and kids to determine the number of hours of quality time he will report. Each week, Jon will ask each of them to give him their number. So, for example, if Jon spends an hour with Cathy and an hour with each of the kids, he will count it as three hours of quality family time.

Step 3: Do

"**Do**" in the Hoshin Plan-Do-Check-Act process is the step where the plan is executed. Take care to build your plan into your daily routine; do not treat it as "something extra" that must be done.

Do: Execute the plan.

Jon begins to incorporate his plans into his Daily Routine. He makes changes in his diet, cutting out simple carbs (carbohydrates) and limiting his fat intake. After talking with his neighbor, a 60-year-old ex-marine who can still pass the Marine Corps Physical Fitness Test for a marine of age 40, Jon reads the Marine Corp Fitness 3X Fitness Program. The "back to the basics" approach of this program fits perfectly with his lifestyle, and he sets aside 30 minutes first thing in the morning, 3 days a week for the workout program. He also begins walking during his lunch hour a couple of days per week and with Cathy most evenings and at least once during the weekend.

Incorporating the plans to improve the quality of his family time proves to be more challenging, but rewarding. He makes every effort to leave the office as often as possible by 5:30 p.m., but it seems more often than not, there is an emergency that keeps him later. On the evenings he does get home early, his kids seem to have homework or plans with friends, so he gets creative. He starts sitting with them when they do their homework. He drives his daughter to and from dance twice a week, and he invites his son's friends over to play basketball. Limiting his Saturdays at work and consolidating out-of-town meetings also gives him more time for family activities. His favorite? The new Sunday afternoon neighborhood volleyball tournaments. Lastly, he schedules date nights with Cathy three months in advance, and makes the plans and reservations right away.

Step 4: Check

Now that you have implemented your plan, you will begin to review and analyze the results. This is where most people fall down. Nearly everyone is horrible at Checking and Adjusting. Stick with this. It is important.

Check: Review and analyze the results; identify what you have learned.

Jon holds a Monthly Review meeting with his family to monitor the plan and check results. He uses the Bowling Chart to help capture and explain his results so far. He is excited to see that he lost 4 lbs. in month 1 versus a target of 2 lbs. And, he spent 42 hours versus a target of 30 with the family. Great news. Cathy and the kids applaud (Figure 1.17).

	Month	1	2	3	4	5	6	7	8	9	10	11	12
Weight Loss Cumulative	Target, in lbs.	–2	–6	–14	–22	–30	–30	–30	–30	–30	–30	–30	–30
	Actual	–4											
Quality Family Time	Target, in hrs.	30	60	60	60	60	60	60	60	60	60	60	60
	Actual	42											

FIGURE 1.17
Jon's Bowling Chart after month 1.

Step 5: Adjust

Based on what you have learned in Step 4, you will now take action based on what you have learned. No problems to solve, no adjustments necessary, full speed ahead.

Adjust: Take action based on what you have learned. Incorporate what you learned (document and standardize), or identify and implement countermeasures.

Back to Step 3: Do

Jon now iterates within the Do-Check-Adjust steps of PDCA cycle. He returns to the Do step and continues to work his plan.

Step 4 Again: Check

He returns to the Check step. He holds a second Monthly Review meeting with his family to monitor the plan and check the results. He uses the Bowling Chart again this month to show his results (Figure 1.18).

Jon lost 4 more pounds. He was now 2 lbs. ahead of the plan. He also spent 73 hours of quality time with his family versus a target of 60. Yeah!

Step 5 Again: Adjust

This time through the cycle, the open discussion during the review meeting identifies a problem. Jon's family cries "uncle" during the Monthly Review, and they ask that he reset his target for quality family time. Jon adjusts his targets based on feedback from his kids. "Dad, we love you, but we need some space. Please lower your target for quality time with us."

Jon lowers his monthly target from 60 to 50 hours after a lot of back and forth discussion with his family (Figure 1.19).

	Month	1	2	3	4	5	6	7	8	9	10	11	12
Weight Loss Cumulative	Target, in lbs.	−2	−6	−14	−22	−30	−30	−30	−30	−30	−30	−30	−30
	Actual	−4	−8										
Quality Family Time	Target, in hrs.	30	60	60	60	60	60	60	60	60	60	60	60
	Actual	42	73										

FIGURE 1.18
Jon's Bowling Chart after month 2.

	Month	1	2	3	4	5	6	7	8	9	10	11	12
Weight Loss Cumulative	Target, in lbs.	-2	-6	-14	-22	-30	-30	-30	-30	-30	-30	-30	-30
	Actual	-4	-8										
Quality Family Time	Target, in hrs.	30	60	60 50	60 50	60 50	60 50	60	60	60	60	60	60
	Actual	42	73										

FIGURE 1.19
Jon's (Revised) Bowling Chart after month 2.

Back to Step 3 Once More: Do

Jon continues to work his plan. He even attends church with his family from time to time.

Step 4 Again: Check

Jon holds a third Monthly Review meeting with his family to monitor the plan and check the results. He again uses the Bowling Chart to show his results (Figure 1.20).

This time, Jon lost 8 lbs. in month 3, putting him 3 lbs. ahead of the plan. And, he spent 55 versus 50 hours of quality time with his family.

	Month	1	2	3	4	5	6	7	8	9	10	11	12
Weight Loss Cumulative	Target, in lbs.	-2	-6	-14	-22	-30	-30	-30	-30	-30	-30	-30	-30
	Actual	-4	-9	-17									
Quality Family Time	Target, in hrs.	30	60	60 50	60 50	60 50	60 50	60 50	60 50	60 50	60 50	60 50	60 50
	Actual	42	73	55									

FIGURE 1.20
Jon's Bowling Chart after month 3.

Step 5 Again: Adjust

With the new, lower Quality Family Time targets, his family is happy. No problems to solve. No changes needed.

Six months into his personal Hoshin journey, Jon reflects on the dramatic changes he made. He not only met his weight loss goal of 30 pounds, but exceeded it by losing 5 pounds more. He enjoyed more quality time with his family, which greatly strengthened their relationship. As he tracked his progress on his Bowling Chart, he thought back to all he learned about Hoshin Kanri through the process. He understood the need to Scan to establish a personal strategy and set strategic directives for himself. He learned about the power of gaining direct feedback, buy-in, and commitment through the Catchball Process. Most of all, he learned the inherent value of the PDCA cycle. Not only did this cycle help him to create his plan, but, importantly, it helped him to stick to it. Several times, he hit plateaus in his weight loss, but through the Check and Adjust process, he was able to make the changes to his diet or switch up his exercise plan to get results over the next cycle. The same was true regarding family time. Jon learned that he had to check and adjust with his wife, and especially his kids. While they loved having him around, teenagers still need their space, so Jon adjusted his objectives and measures accordingly.

Throughout the personal Hoshin journey, Jon drew the obvious parallels to how he could use the process in his business. He remembered a business card that the gentleman had given him along with the Hoshin Kanri for Personal Change book. He then reached out and received the book that would change his business.

KEY TAKEAWAYS FROM CHAPTER 1

There is a lot of work to be done before starting the Hoshin Kanri (strategy deployment) process. Remember the lengthy "Scan" step before you got to PDCA?

1. YOUR GAPS

   Take it seriously. This is your life. Invest some time working through the Scan step to identify your most important gaps. Spending time and energy to try to make a change that doesn't really matter to you is dumb.

2. YOUR TEAM

   You need to get your key constituents (Jon's family in Chapter 1) *aligned* with you. Remember the bacon and egg breakfast story? You want them involved, but better yet, you want them committed. You want them to have some ownership in your personal change.

3. CATCHBALL

   Use the Catchball process to have some frank conversations with your key constituents. Listen to them and adjust when you know they are right.

4. PRIORITIZE

   Use a process to prioritize. Remember to select the "Important" versus the "Urgent" for inclusion on your short list. Make use of the Interrelationship Digraph. It is an extremely powerful tool and it is not nearly as complicated as it looks.

5. FOCUS

   Limit your critical few objectives (your personal Hoshins). I say three or less, especially when you are just starting out.

6. PDCA CYCLE

   "Plan" is fairly easy, and the "Do" step often happens. It's the "Check" and "Adjust" steps that often fall by the wayside. Stick with it. They are critical.

7. BOWLING CHART

   Use the chart to keep track of your progress. Do it; it works.

REFERENCES

1. Jackson, T. L. 2006. *Hoshin Kanri for the Lean enterprise: Developing competitive capabilities and managing profit*. Boca Raton, FL: CRC Press, pp. 1–2.
2. Akao, Y. ed. 1991. *Introduction to Hoshin Kanri: Policy deployment for successful TQM*. (translated by Glenn Mazur) New York: Productivity Press, p. xxv.

2

Hoshin Kanri to Deploy Business Strategy

I expect to spend the rest of my life in the future, so I want to be reasonably sure of what kind of future it's going to be. That is my reason for planning.

Charles Kettering

Vision without execution is hallucination.

Thomas A. Edison

Alice came to a fork in the road. "Which road do I take?" she asked. "Where do you want to go?" responded the Cheshire cat. "I don't know," Alice answered. "Then," said the cat, "it doesn't matter."

Lewis Carroll[1]

JON'S BUSINESS

Jon had inherited a very complicated business challenge in his new role as president at IGC Aerospace. Bottom line, he was issued a personal challenge by the chairman to increase profit and cash, while the revenue line was expected to be flat, at best. In addition, his business unit did not make safety a priority. He received at least three calls at home last month regarding dangerous safety "near misses." His vice president of operations resented him because he had been in consideration for Jon's job, and, on top of all of this, he had inherited 24—yes, 24—simultaneous strategic initiatives from his predecessor, all of which were in process. Finally, Jon knew that his failure to provide results would not only impact the security of his job, but also those of his staff.

In order to get the results that his boss and IGC's board expected, he had to make some significant improvements in business performance. So, at the end of a weekly staff meeting, he handed every staff member a copy of The Little Book of Hoshin: A tool for business change. *He informed them that, starting the next week, they would work through the book during daily lunchtime staff meetings for the next few weeks to turn the situation around. (He also moved the daily walks on his calendar to before work every morning during this time.) He requested that they read ahead and come prepared with their ideas. Jon thought he got a lot of eye rolling at his first family Catchball meeting, but his staff's response to* The Little Hoshin Book *was priceless.*

Much like the book for personal change that he had first been given, this book was very simple, with no publisher information or table of contents, only a simple title page. Again, it opened with an explanation of Hoshin Kanri, but expounded on the importance of the strategy formulation work that precedes Hoshin. Basically, it included an extended version of the Scan section in the personal book. This is where Jon and his team started.

INTRODUCTION TO *THE LITTLE BOOK*

Hoshin Kanri is a powerful process used in business. The words *Hoshin* and *Kanri* have been translated to mean a number of things. A common definition in English is **strategy deployment,** and you often see a compass used as the image to represent the term.

The subject of Strategy Deployment (Hoshin Kanri) is not simple, but, in comparison, the subject of **Strategy Formulation** is an immense and incredibly complex thing. Experts and authors cannot even seem to agree on the definitions of the terms used within the science and art called *strategy formulation*. Even the word *strategy* itself is sometimes treated as a "how" by some experts and authors, while others see it as a "what."

Hoshin Kanri: A strategy deployment tool, approach, or system. It is an element of a larger management system introduced to the western world in the 1980s as Total Quality Management (TQM).

Total Quality Management (TQM): A management system with a misleading name. The name is a misnomer because the system actually encompasses all elements of an organization, not just quality. TQM is considered to be an out-of-date term by some, but the author believes that the concepts remain valid to this day. This belief is supported by the fact that several organizations are employing TQM and Hoshin Kanri with great success as of this writing.

For purposes of strategy deployment, we are going to be looking for one thing as a result of the often byzantine strategy formulation process—a set of breakthrough strategic objectives that need to be deployed into the organization. These "vital few" breakthrough objectives also are called *Critical Few Objectives*, and *Hoshin Objectives*, or just plain *Hoshins*. You get the picture.

That's it. Just a few objectives (or "whats") that the organization needs to deploy and execute. It seems simple enough, but trust me, a good, short list of Hoshins is not easy to come by.

Hoshin Kanri consultants, who assist organizations with Hoshin, report a surprising number of organizations preparing to deploy a strategy when they don't really have one. Or, if they do have a strategy, it is often not very sound.

It is critical to determine a strategic direction before embarking on a strategy deployment. Some organizations call it their "True North." So, before we get into the steps of Hoshin Kanri (i.e., strategy deployment), we are going to first use the Scan process for *creating* a business strategy as a part of this exercise. We will then walk through the start of the Plan-Do-Check-Adjust (PDCA) in the Hoshin Kanri process with a business application.

Strategy Deployment: A process that follows Strategy Formulation. It uses the key objectives (e.g., the Hoshins) that were developed in the Strategy Formulation process and makes them available for review and action throughout the organization, both vertically down through the organization's layers and across the organization's functions.

Strategy Formulation: A process where strategy is created or revised.

Strategy: Within the confines of this little book is an overall approach to achieve what an organization proclaims in its purpose statements (Vision, Mission, Values), to include the determination of its strategic objectives.

Step 1: Scan (The Strategy Formulation process)
Step 2: Plan (the Hoshin Kanri process begins)
Step 3: Do
Step 4: Check
Step 5: Adjust

Step 1: Scan

This first step, Scan, is about taking some steps to identify a few key objectives in support of your strategy.[2] It presupposes that the organization has done some strategy formulation work in the recent past that included an examination of both external and internal influences on strategy to include:

- The external environment
- Industry attractiveness
- Your competitors
- Your value chain
- Your capabilities and competencies
- Your competitive advantage

This step starts with understanding where you are today and where you want to be a few years from now.

The Scan Process

1. Develop your Mission Statement
2. Define your Values
3. Define your Current State
4. Define your Vision
5. Design your Desired Future State
6. Identify the gaps between the Future and Current States
7. Prioritize the gaps; define your Business Priorities

The First Working Lunch Meeting

The first working lunch did not go as well as planned. To sum it up, it was a disaster. The idea of Hoshin Kanri was met with considerable suspicion, and when talk shifted to reducing the number of strategic initiatives, no one wanted to give up the ones they considered to be "theirs." Especially resistant was Jon's vice president of operations, who owned five initiatives, all focused on cost reduction. Though Jon pointed out the need to also focus on safety, quality, and on-time delivery, his staff rallied together again (unfortunately, against Jon), arguing that cost reduction needed to be the focus next year to achieve the very aggressive profit and cash targets.

This meeting opened Jon's eyes. To make the changes needed to improve performance, he had to overcome his staff's resistance. He had to get them in his corner. Jon had attended a change management seminar led by Jeanenne LaMarsh a few years back. Because he had been so impressed with the process, he reached out to her for help.

In their conversation, Jon explained that, while reading The Little Book of Hoshin *for personal change, he had used a very simple Current State/ Desired Future State model to help him clarify his personal change plan, but his situation at IGC Aerospace called for a different approach. The situation at IGC was far more complicated. He described the significant resistance he was facing and shared his desire to use Hoshin Kanri as a tool to help drive change in his new organization.*

Jeanenne explained that the LaMarsh Managed Change™ (www.lamarsh.com) methodology and Hoshin Kanri complement one another very well. She explained that the methodology not only defines an organization's Current State and Desired Future State, but also identifies and mitigates resistance within highly skeptical organizations, like the one Jon described.

The Second Working Lunch Meeting

The second working lunch went somewhat better than the first. Together, Jon and his staff began walking through the Scan process in the little Hoshin workbook, which was in some ways similar to the Personal Change workbook, yet more complex for use in a business environment. Before defining the Current State and the Desired Future State, the workbook explained the importance of creating a mission statement, defining the organization's values and vision statement, and completing an external and internal analysis to help define the current reality.

Jon decided that, rather than "reinvent the wheel," it would be best to start by examining what IGC Aerospace had already created. He posted summaries from the previous year's strategic planning documents on the wall for review. He pointed out that in the previous year the focus was on understanding the strategic environment and on formulating strategy and a set of strategic objectives. The strategic objectives had been translated into 24 strategic initiatives and basically "tossed out" to the organization for implementation. And, this they had to do along with their daily workload and departmental and individual objectives—a recipe for disaster. His people all nodded to show their agreement. Jon added that the remainder of this year and next year would be about reviewing what was developed last year and deploying, in a more effective and efficient manner, a set of critical, breakthrough objectives. He drew a big rectangle covering his white board and labeled it Environment. *Inside the larger rectangle, he drew a slightly smaller rectangle and labeled it* IGC Aerospace. *Jon told them that this year they were going to briefly review what was developed last year, but spend most of their time looking inside IGC Aerospace. With this new perspective in mind, they began to develop the Mission Statement (Figure 2.1).*

FIGURE 2.1
The focus is *inside* IGC Aerospace.

1: Develop Your Mission Statement

The **Mission Statement** defines who you are as an organization, what business you are in, and what value you provide. A typical mission statement might include comments about the key constituents, such as customers, shareholders, employees, suppliers, and the communities within which you reside. It also might include comments about industries, product, and service offerings.

> **Mission:** Who are we? What business are we in? Our present main activities? What value do we provide?

Define Your Mission:
We make high quality components and subsystems for the aerospace industry. Our success will ensure that customers will build their business, employees will build their futures, and shareholders will build their wealth.

After some discussion, the IGC Aerospace team agreed to stick with the Mission Statement they had created the previous year with the help of the hugely expensive consultants.

2: Develop/Define Your Values

Values are the guiding principles of an organization that communicate the expected collective norms and behavior of everyone in the organization. In other words, Values serve as the basis for making decisions within the organization and act as the foundation for communication with colleagues and customers.

> *Values:* Guiding principles, the expected collective norms and behavior of everybody in the organization.

The prior president at IGC Aerospace had been a bit of an autocrat and had imposed his own Basic Beliefs on the organization, but very few in the organization had really "owned them." With input and agreement from the entire staff, Jon and his team chose the following values, in which each felt invested and obligated to uphold.

- **Safety:** Our foundational value. We care for our employees.
- **Performance:** We measure results and reward achievement.
- **Integrity:** We uphold trustworthiness and business ethics.
- **Respect:** We value everyone, and we lead with humility.
- **Innovation:** We encourage creativity.
- **Teamwork:** We work together to succeed.

Collectively they spelled S.P.I.R.I.T.

Jon concluded the second meeting with a sense of accomplishment. Great strides had not been made, but they did come together in agreement over a few things. He would take that.

The Third Working Lunch Meeting

3: Define Your Current State

Take a step back to consider your environment, your current situation, your **Current State**, if you will. For this exercise, you will use an **Affinity Diagram**, which is a tool used to help organize ideas generated in brainstorming or problem-solving meetings. You will first list as many observations as possible about your current state, and then you will classify each statement into one of five categories: Structure, Process, People, Culture, or Metrics (Figure 2.2).

Current State: Our current reality.

Affinity Diagram: A tool used to help organize ideas generated in brainstorming or problem-solving meetings.

Structure	Process
People	Culture
Metrics	

FIGURE 2.2
Categories used to define the current state.

As everyone walked into the conference room for their third lunch-time working session, they noticed a large, blank whiteboard with Modified Affinity Diagram *written at the top. When Jon asked who was familiar with this tool, he was met with blank stares. He explained that an Affinity Diagram is a tool used to help organize ideas generated in brainstorming or problem-solving meetings. Ideas with an affinity for one another are grouped together by category. In this case, the categories have been provided in advance and the ideas are to be placed in the provided categories.*

Referring to The Little Book, *Jon described the process. He motioned to the pads of sticky notes in front of each staff member and asked that they use as many as they needed to describe the current situation at IGC Aerospace, sticking them on the board as they go. He emphasized that the descriptions need not be negative or positive, just honest observations. When the activity finally died down, Jon looked with pride at the whiteboard, which was covered with notes of all colors.*

He then stepped to another whiteboard, divided the board into four rectangles and wrote the words Structure, Process, People, *and* Culture *in the four boxes. Near the bottom of board, he wrote* Metrics.

He handed each of them a list of brief definitions (Figure 2.3).

Next, he asked his staff to work together to place each sticky note into one of the five categories shown on the whiteboard. They got right to work and were soon working together and seemed to be thoroughly enjoying the process.

- PROCESS
  - How we do work
- STRUCTURE
  - Organization structure, systems
- PEOPLE
  - Skills and competencies
- CULTURE
  - Beliefs, behaviors, rules (written and unwritten)
- METRICS
  - What we measure and how we measure it

Source: www.LaMarsha.com

FIGURE 2.3
Definitions used in LaMarsh Change Management™ Methodology.

When they finished, Jon thanked them for their excellent work. He noticed more camaraderie among the team and more excitement with the process. He explained that in the following meeting they would take the next step. They would define the Desired Future State of the business, and he asked that again, they come prepared to share their ideas.

The Fourth Working Lunch Meeting

Jon's staff entered his office with smiles on their faces. Most of them had enjoyed the Current State exercise, and he hoped they would be equally energized for their work today. A few of them even carried their copy of The Little Book with them. They noticed the modified Affinity Diagram again, now blank, and a blown-up picture of the previous meeting's diagram hanging on the adjacent wall (Figure 2.4).

Jon started the meeting by welcoming everyone in attendance and thanking them for what they had accomplished the day before. He reminded them that today's exercise was about designing their Desired Future State, and that the first step to this was to create the vision.

4: Define Your Vision

For an organization, **vision** is the picture of the future, i.e., where the business is going. For a business, vision is a picture of the future that might include things, such as customers, employees, sales,

Vision: Our dream for the future. It's our "picture" of the future.

IGC Aerospace's Current State	
STRUCTURE xxxxxxxxxx	**PROCESS** xxxxxxxxxx
PEOPLE xxxxxxxxxx	**CULTURE** xxxxxxxxxx
METRICS:	

FIGURE 2.4
IGC Aerospace's Current State.

profit, suppliers, community relationships, structure, process, people, culture, and metrics. This "picture" might include words, such as *global, leader, premier, most respected*, or *successful*.

Define Your Vision:
To become the most successful aerospace manufacturing company in the world.

After much deliberation, the IGC Aerospace team agreed that the Vision they had worked so hard to create just a few months earlier was still an accurate picture of IGC's desired, ultimate future.

5: Your Desired Future State

As we head toward our vision, our **Desired Future State** is our expectation for where we should be at a specific point in time.

> **Desired Future State:** As we head toward our Vision, this is our expectation for where we should be at a specific point in time. For example, five years from today.

For this exercise, pick a point in time a few years from now. Think about what you like about your Current State diagram and what you dislike about it. Now, bring the favorable things forward into your Future State diagram. These are the things you want to retain as you move forward making changes in your organization.

Consider again each facet of the Future State diagram. In terms of structure, process, people, and culture, ask yourself (based on any strategy formulation work you concluded recently and the strategic objectives that came out of that process): Where do we need to be in five years? Where do we need to be with all of these things? What is your Desired Future State? Once again, try to quantify or think about how you will measure these things. For example, if your Desired Future State involves improving employee satisfaction, how will you measure it? What metric(s) will you use?

A lot of what showed up in the Current State was negative, but not all of it. One of their challenges was to identify the positive aspects in the Current State that should be carried forward into the Future State. Using the modified Affinity Diagram process again, Jon asked his staff to review the Current State comments, and then use the sticky notes again to describe how they want the Future State to look. He told them to include both the favorable aspects from the current situation that they would like to carry forward, as well as the changes they would like to make. The team studied the Current

IGC Aerospace's Desired Future State As of date: 5 Years from Today	
STRUCTURE xxxxxxxxxx	**PROCESS** xxxxxxxxxx
PEOPLE xxxxxxxxxx	**CULTURE** xxxxxxxxxx
METRICS:	

FIGURE 2.5
IGC's Desired Future State Worksheet: As of date: Five years from today.

State, and then busily jotted down notes and stuck them in the corresponding category (Structure, Process, People, Culture, Metrics) on the whiteboard, now labeled Desired Future State.

After an hour, the activity started to slow. Jon watched as his staff members walked back and forth in front of the board, reading the comments that had been posted by their teammates. Many nodded as they read the words written by others. He hoped they would bring the same energy to the next meeting. It would likely be a long one.

Earlier that afternoon, he had checked in with Jeanenne to update her on their progress. She reminded him that once he and his team agreed on the Current State and the Desired Future State, the next step would be to identify the biggest "gaps" requiring closure. What were the critical few things that must change? In other words, the team would be working to establish their Hoshin Objectives, or **Hoshins** *(Figure 2.5).*

Hoshins: The critical few or the BIG, "breakthrough" objectives.

The Fifth Working Lunch Meeting

6: Identify the Gaps

Take some time to compare your Current State and your Desired Future State. Now, identify the "gaps." A **gap** is a difference between the Current State and the Future State, i.e., things that will require change.

Gaps: The difference between the Current State and the Future State. Things that will require change.

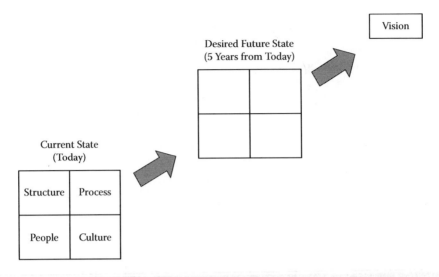

FIGURE 2.6
The change: From Current State to Desired Future State, toward the Vision.

If you have a lot of gaps, you need to consider which ones are the most significant. What are the biggest, most important gaps that separate your organization's reality from the vision?

As Figure 2.6 shows, change will be required to move from the Current State to the Desired Five-Year Future State, all while heading toward the organization's vision.

Friday's extended lunch session started with a review of the Current State and Desired Future State diagrams. Jon now had both diagrams blown up and posted side-by-side on the conference room wall. He asked the team to take the next hour to look for the big gaps between the two (Figure 2.7). He asked that they try their best to consider the differences between the Desired

Identifying the Gaps Worksheet
List your biggest gaps, in no particular order:
Jon and team listed 45 major Gaps!

FIGURE 2.7
Identifying the Gaps worksheet.

Future State and the Current State that were most important to the organization as a whole.

*Now, Jon reminded them that they were already working on 24 strategic initiatives, and he posted the list of these initiatives on the wall. He expressed the need to find a way to group and then prioritize the gaps they needed to close, while also considering the major projects already underway. The lead Lean Six Sigma Master black belt on Jon's staff suggested that they use an **Interrelationship Digraph**—a Cause and Effect Diagram that helps identify drivers and outcomes (Figure 2.8). The drivers become candidates for Hoshins.*

Interrelationship Digraph: Sometimes called the Root Cause tool, because it helps identify the hidden causes. It shows the cause and effect relationships and helps to analyze the links between different aspects of a complex situation.

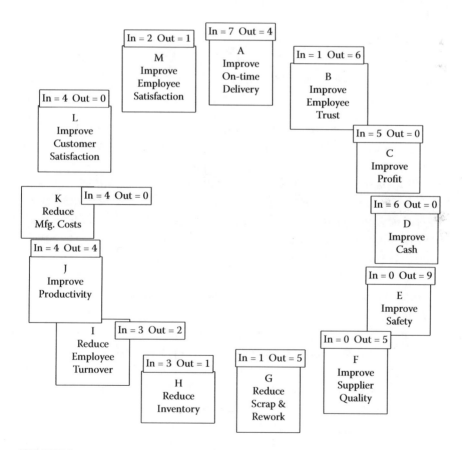

FIGURE 2.8
Interrelationship Digraph (see Appendix B).

DRIVERS:

E: *Improve Safety (9)*
B: *Improve Employee Trust (6)*
F: *Improve Supplier Quality (5)*
G: *Reduce Scrap and Rework (5)*

> **Driver:** The elements in an Interrelationship Digraph with the most outgoing arrows are causes. They also might be root causes.

As a result of the analysis performed involving several processes, 12 candidates still remained as potential Hoshins for the next year. A decision had to be made. Jon asked that each one of his staff members, by Monday morning, review the list of 12 Drivers and choose their top five, only five, and e-mail them to him in ranked order. For example, the no. 1 Driver is the gap they believe is the most critical to close, the no. 2 Driver would be the second priority, and so on. Jon would make the ultimate decision, but he wanted to base his decision on their input.

The group surprised Jon by breaking out into applause.

The Sixth Working Lunch Meeting

7: Your Priorities

Now that you have defined your Gaps, it's time to prioritize them. You can't change everything in the business at once, so you need to decide where you will focus for the next 12 months.

The team assembled again in Jon's office. By now, the group was working together comfortably, with the exception of his vice president of operations. It had become apparent that he had no interest in the process and did not care for Jon's leadership style. Jon came to realize that he would soon have to transition this vice president out and find a replacement.

As everyone settled in, Jon asked for their Top Five lists, and he charted them on his whiteboard. The voting showed quite a bit of consensus.

Jon considered what to do about the final list, and once again with the help of his Lean Six Sigma Master black belt, he created a Priority Matrix. For each issue, the team assigned a 1 to 10 ranking to indicate: Importance to the Customer, Gap in Performance, Significance to Long-Term Plan, and Urgency. By summing A + B + C + D, a total point value was obtained and used to rank the issues. In the example in Figure 2.9, Issue X ranked at the top of the priority list with 35 total points.

Jon explained that when they started the Interrelationship Digraph with Employee Satisfaction and Employee Engagement as the desired outcomes,

PRIORITY MATRIX FOR SELECTING "HOSHINS"
EVALUATION CRITERIA

Issue	(A) Importance to Customer 10 = VERY 1 = NOT	(B) Gap in Performance 10 = HUGE 1 = NONE	(C) Significance to long-term plan 10 = VERY 1 = NOT	(D) Urgency 10 = VERY 1 = NONE	(E) Total = (A)+(B) +(C)+(D)	Rank Based on points in column (E)
Z	8	10	5	5	28	2
X	10	10	10	5	35	1
V	5	7	8	6	26	4
W	1	10	5	5	21	5
Y	4	10	6	7	27	3

FIGURE 2.9
Priority matrix for selecting "Hoshins."

Safety was found to be the Driver, i.e., the place to start. Hence, Hoshin no. 1 was about Safety.

When they started the Interrelationship Digraph with Customer Satisfaction as the desired outcome, Quality (supplier quality, to be more precise) was found to be the Driver, i.e., the place to start. Hence, Hoshin no. 2 was about Quality.

In the book *Beyond Strategic Vision*, Michael Cowley and Ellen Domb describe the "Three Ds" approach, a tool to help organizations reduce initiatives to a manageable number.[3]

1. Can we delete it?
2. Can we defer it?
3. Should we delegate it?

and, in some cases

4. Just do it (if it fits into the plan and it is obvious that something needs to be done) or finish it (if it fits into the plan and we are near the finish line).

Using this approach, Jon and his team decided to finish two strategic initiatives that were almost complete. They deleted six, deferred eight, delegated four, and four of the strategic initiatives readily folded into and supported their two Hoshins.

```
┌─────────────────────────────────────────────────┐
│                                                   │
│   IGC'S CHANGE PRIORITIES (The "Hoshins")         │
│                                                   │
│   1. Improve Safety—make it a value at AGC        │
│   2. Improve Supplier Quality                     │
│                                                   │
└─────────────────────────────────────────────────┘
```

FIGURE 2.10
IGC's change priorities.

Jon explained to the team that for the next year, they would apply the Four Ds to most of the preexisting strategic initiatives and focus on the two things that were most impacting employee and customer satisfaction: Safety and Quality. For those who expressed concern about cost, Jon explained that cost would come (Figure 2.10).

In the back of his mind, Jon remembered what a boss from early in his career used to say: "Make Safety and Quality priority no. 1 and no. 2 and Delivery and Cost will almost always take care of themselves." Jon had seen many examples during his career that had confirmed his boss' wisdom.

Step 2: Plan

Make sure to keep the S.M.A.R.T. criteria in mind when defining your objectives.

Specific: Explain *what* in clear terms
Measureable: Quantify or at least suggest an indicator of progress
Assignable: Specify *who* will do it
Realistic: Within a practical range of achievement
Time-related: Specify *when* the result(s) can be achieved

Jon and the team applied the S.M.A.R.T. criteria to the Hoshins and created Planning Worksheets (Figure 2.11).

Objective (Hoshin) #2: Improve Supplier Quality from 94 to 99 percent in 12 months
Measures: Percent of Supplier receipts accepted, identify some leading indicators (Figure 2.12 and Figure 2.13)

Planning Worksheet

Objective (Hoshin) #1: Change behaviors by making safety the #1 "Value" at IGC Aerospace

Measures: Employee surveys, leading indicator metrics, safety results

Means (HOW)	Measures	WHEN/WHO
1. xxx xxxxx xxx	Xxx	Xxxx
2. xxxxxx xxxxx	Xxx	Xxx
3. xxxx xx xxxx		

FIGURE 2.11
IGC's plan for change no. 1.

Means (HOW)	Measures	WHEN/WHO
1. xxx xxxxx xxx	Xxx	Xxxx
2. xxxxxxxx xxxx	Xxx	Xxx
3. xxxx xx xxxx		

FIGURE 2.12
IGC's plan for change no. 2.

	Month	1	2	3	4	5	6	7	8	9	10	11	12
xxxxx	Target in xxx	Xx	xx	xx	xx	xx	xx	xx	Xx	Xx	xx	xx	xx
	Actual												
xxxxx	Target in xxx	Xx	xx	xx	xx	xx	xx	xx	Xx	Xx	xx	xx	xx
	Actual												

FIGURE 2.13
IGC's Bowling Chart.

Catchball

*So far, the Hoshin process has motivated only the senior leaders in the organization. Jon realized it was time to engage others in the process by using the **Catchball** process. The diagram for the process in* The Little Book for Business Change *is a little complex, but it involves a fairly simple concept (Figure 2.14).*

Catchball: An interactive process of tossing items and possibilities back and forth like a game of "catch." It sometimes results in changes to proposed objectives, means, and measures.

The Leadership team meets with people at the next lower level to toss ideas back and forth in the catchball process.

Let's say at the leadership level, the Objective (the What) is "Improve safety and make safety a Value at IGC" and the Means (the How) is determined to be "Focus the organization on safety-related behaviors versus the results."

When this cascades to the middle management level, "Focus the organization on safety-related behaviors versus the results" becomes the Objective (the What) and "Design and roll out a new Gain Share program that rewards employees for the 'right' safety behaviors" is determined to be the Means (the How).

When this cascades to the line management level, "Design and roll out a new Gain Share program that rewards employees for the 'right' safety behaviors" becomes the Objective (the What) and "Ensure that employees are exhibiting the 'right' safety behaviors" is determined to be the Means (the How).

At each point in the cascade process, Catchball is used to discuss the objectives, means, and measures. Are they realistic? Are they achievable? How should the objective be met? How should results be measured? What targets should be set?

The cascading process continues, eventually reaching the working (shop floor) level (Figure 2.14).

Jon is ready for the next little book.

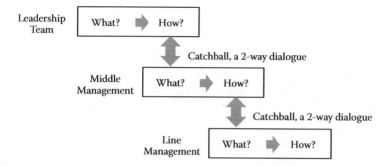

FIGURE 2.14
The Cascade process, with Catchball.

KEY TAKEAWAYS FROM CHAPTER 2

Here are a few of the main takeaways from Chapter 2 of this book.

1. HAVE A STRATEGY
   Before you consider embarking on the Hoshin Kanri journey, make sure you have a strategy worthy of deployment. Mission and Vision statements are not enough. The Hoshin process will look for some "meaty" objectives upon which to "chew." Spending time and money deploying a bad strategy (or less than impactful objectives) is not smart.

2. INVOLVE YOUR TEAM
   You need to get your key constituents (Jon's staff in Chapter 2) *aligned* with you. Remember the bacon and egg breakfast story? You want them involved, but better yet, you want them committed with you in the change. You want them to have some ownership.

3. APPLY ORGANIZATIONAL CHANGE MANAGEMENT
   Within an organization, there is always some resistance to any change, and I do mean ANY change. You could offer to give everyone in the business $1,000 in cash, and you still would have a few resisters/detractors. Organizational Change Management (OCM) is a methodology/set of tools designed to help identify and mitigate resistance. Jon needed to use OCM to help explain and "sell" the idea of using Hoshin Kanri within the business. He also will continue to use it on a project-by-project basis to help eliminate the resistance to some of the more significant change projects that flow from the Hoshin objectives.

4. EMPLOY CATCHBALL

Use the Catchball process to have some frank conversations with your staff, and for your staff to have similar conversations with their people, and so on.

5. PRIORITIZE (AND DESELECT)

Use a process to prioritize. Use tools like the Interrelationship Digraph to help identify the Drivers from the Outcomes. Use a Prioritization Matrix to include some data in your prioritization process. If nothing else, apply the "Important" versus the "Urgent" test to your short list.

6. FOCUS! FOCUS! FOCUS!

Limit your critical few objectives (your Hoshins) to three or less, especially when you are just starting out.

7. STICK WITH THE PLAN-DO-CHECK-ADJUST (PDCA) CYCLE

"Plan" is fairly easy, and the "Do" step often happens. It's the Check and Adjust steps that often fall by the wayside. Stick with it. They are critical.

8. USE THE BOWLING CHART

Use the Bowling Chart to keep track of your progress.

9. INVESTIGATE THE X-MATRIX AND THE A3 REPORTS

The X-Matrix and A3 are outside the scope of the short stories included in this little book, but most Hoshin Kanri deployments make use of them. See Appendix C for some information on the basics. In addition, the Recommended Reading List section of this book includes great resources for both tools.

REFERENCES

1. Carroll, L. 2000. *Alice's adventures in wonderland and through the looking glass.* New York: Signet Classic Printing.
2. Jackson, T. L. 2006. *Hoshin Kanri for the Lean enterprise: Developing competitive capabilities and managing profit.* Boca Raton, FL: CRC Press, pp. 1–2.
3. Cowley, M., and E. Domb. 1997. *Beyond strategic vision: Effective corporate action with Hoshin planning.* New York: Routledge, p. 95.

3

Interviews with Hoshin Kanri Experts

By three methods we may learn wisdom: First, by reflection, which is noblest; second, by imitation, which is easiest; and third, by experience, which is bitterest.

Confucius

You cannot create experience. You must undergo it.

Albert Camus

Experience is simply a name we give our mistakes.

Oscar Wilde

INTRODUCTION TO CHAPTER 3

What follows is the result of numerous interviews with Hoshin Kanri experts—practitioners in industry, consultants, authors, and professors. Many of these experts were on the ground at Hewlett-Packard, Danaher Corporation, and Florida Power & Light when Hoshin Kanri was first implemented in the United States. Others have deep personal experience with Toyota. I've scoured through countless pages of notes from my interviews and have included some of the most insightful responses about successes and failures with Hoshin. I hope you will find their comments as fascinating as did I. Listed below are the contents of this chapter.

WHAT IS HOSHIN KANRI?

Joe Colletti: Hoshin Kanri is primarily a visual deployment system for strategic planning. Hoshin's greatest power is that it creates visual templates at each level of the organization that connect the plan down through the organization in such a way that you can ensure alignment of individuals across the organization, both vertically and horizontally. It lets you see where you're going, and it puts you in a position to monitor things and work together effectively. It's powerful!

Hoshin is fundamentally all about creating and leveraging visibility around your plan.

Lisa Boisvert: A strategic planning practice that defines a direction and priorities, aligns the organization around that direction through dialog and detailed plans, then implements and measures against those plans in a disciplined way.

Mara Melum: Hoshin Planning is a system that helps leaders identify the most important goal to break through to new heights of success and then to align the organization so there is deep and broad engagement to achieve the breakthrough goal.

Larry Rubrich: It's a way of connecting an organization's goals with the Lean tools to achieve those goals.

Tom Cluley: The Hoshin process helps the entire organization align by setting strategic objectives and metrics that are key performance metrics, instead of just performance metrics that measure the performance of the organization against the objectives of the organization. The alignment helps to create the focus. It's the Hoshin needle, so it gives organizations their true north.

Tom Jackson: Have you heard of the Balanced Scorecard? It was derived from Hoshin Kanri. Hoshin has been around for a long time … and people use it. They use pieces of it and aren't aware of it. You've heard of the Malcolm Baldridge Award and the Shingo Prize? Those prizes are based upon Hoshin Kanri. You may not have heard the term *Hoshin Kanri*, but you're probably familiar with some of the techniques that have been derived from it. You've probably also heard of the Plan-Do-Check-Act cycles or the Deming cycles. Most people in manufacturing have heard of it. This is the scientific method, right? Hoshin, a.k.a., Strategy

Deployment, is just an application of the scientific method. It's a way to execute strategy.

A. Blanton Godfrey: It's a way of taking strategic goals and turning them into action items. Key strategies support the organization's vision, and from strategies come goals, which must be measurable, and from goals come actions.

Jeffrey Liker: It's a method for deciding the strategic direction from the top and then cascading that down to goals and objectives and then the means to achieve those goals and objectives.

David Silverstein: I think Hoshin gets confused too often with being about both creating and executing strategy. It's really just about executing strategy. Strategy is the input to Hoshin. We need to keep Hoshin focused on strategy execution and implementation.

Lois Gold: Hoshin Kanri is about making and cascading objectives and metrics.

Bruce Sheridan: On the Hoshin side, you start by considering the environment you are in, then you develop your Vision, Mission, and Long-Term Strategy. You also develop a One-Year Tactical Agenda. We found at Florida Power & Light that the One-Year Tactical Agenda should be based on a rolling 12 months, and not tied to the fiscal calendar.

On the Kanri side, the governance side, it's where you manage getting the strategic plan accomplished. We held, at a minimum, monthly meetings to review the Hoshin plan, the progress we had made, where we were falling short. And, then, whenever we saw that we were falling short, we would decide what to do. Did we need to start a Design for Six Sigma project, a Lean project, or a problem-solving project? You had to get financial approval and approval from a master black belt regarding the approach to take. We let the strategy drive the projects we were going to work. We found the gaps, i.e., where we were missing the strategic plan, then we launched projects to close the gaps. Over time, we got the whole company aligned to our corporate strategies, and our corporate dashboards and metrics. All of our Lean Six Sigma projects were 100-percent aligned with the strategy. It helped move FP&L from being considered one of the worst performing utilities to one of the best. And, then, people wanted to come visit us—in droves.

Paul Docherty: I would say it's about aligning your organization to execute with purpose to achieve a few key things that matter to you strategically.

Gerhard Plenert: Hoshin Kanri is a strategic planning and management tool focused on the expertise of the individual. It integrates the individual tribal knowledge into a strategic map. The goal is to create an organization focused strategically on quality. It uses a mapping process that integrates the collective thinking power of all employees to create an organization that is the best in its field. Hoshin is a management system wherein all employees participate, from the top down and from the bottom up. It creates goals, identifies control points and milestones, and links daily control activities to company strategy.

Wes Waldo: Hoshin Kanri is a process for consistently achieving breakthrough objectives and turning them into daily practice.

Michele Bechtell: Hoshin is a proven methodology to reliably achieve radical changes in measurable strategic levels of performance (covered in my book, *The Management Compass* (AMACOM, 1995)).

A key stumbling block in experiencing the power of Hoshin is infrequent review with timely corrective action. The solution is adherence to a simple set of disciplined review protocols that routinely communicate deviations from plan, accelerate factual gap analysis, and verify sufficient corrective action. Frequent factual review is common sense. Doing it in group formation requires disciplined protocols for coordination (covered in my book, *On Target: How to Conduct Effective Business Reviews* (Berrett-Koehler Publishers, 2002)).

Once learned, Hoshin becomes a way of life. It applies to the workplace, civic government, charitable organizations, and personal life management.

In many ways, implementing Hoshin is like learning to ride a bike. The first year, the simple mechanics promise distance, speed, and choice destinations, yet coordinating the mechanics initially feels awkward; the objective is to climb on and stay on the bike despite a few spills and skinned knees along the way. The second year, the conscious repeat of each action becomes familiar and self-reinforcing with a focus on gears, balance, and coordination. The third year, the rider no longer thinks about the mechanics of the bike, rather the focus is on purpose, destination, and speed, not the mechanics of the transport. And, once learned, one never forgets it. Now think of a group of novice bikers at different locations aiming for a continually changing sequence of destinations with variable weather conditions.

Many people believe that Hoshin cannot be implemented before gaining company-wide skills, such as factual root cause problem solving and continuous process improvement. Not true. Hoshin can be implemented at the same time to great effect. It can be used to accelerate company-wide acquisition of such skills to achieve strategic imperatives.

THREE WORDS TO DESCRIBE HOSHIN KANRI?

I asked the experts to describe Hoshin Kanri using only three words. The words used most frequently are shown in Figure 3.1.

Greg Watson: Catchball, Coordination, and "Self-regulating responsibility management." I know that the last is not a single word, but I don't know a good word to express the idea.
Michael Bremer: Focus on importance.
David Silverstein: Structured, Strategy, Execution.
Lois Gold: Accountability, Transparency, Alignment.

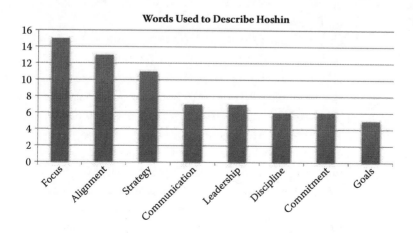

FIGURE 3.1
Three words to describe Hoshin Kanri.

Rafeek Kottai: Direction, Alignment, Communication.

Barry Witcher: Manage, Purpose, Focus.

Mara Melum: Breakthrough, Alignment, Engagement.

Kevin Meyer: Aligning the Future.

Gary Vance: Structure, Involvement, Disciplined follow-through.

Bob King: Hoshin saved P & G $2 billion!

James Hinkle: Strategy. Support. Execution. Communication.

Wes Waldo: Stretch. Structure. Sustainment.

Mark Caponigro: End in Mind.

Mark Caponigro: All Together Now.

Bob Emiliani: Process. Practice. Patience.

Jane Dwyer: Clear vision. Focus. Alignment.

Zane Ferry: Catchball. Patience. Commitment.

Rafeek Kottai: Effective Strategy Implementation.

John Gaul: Strategy, Alignment, Transformation.

Adrian Mulder: Interactive, Breakthrough, and Follow-up.

Lisa Boisvert: Focused, Hardworking, Measurable.

Thom Williams: Approach, Deployment, Results.

Chandrashekhar Kulkarni: Strategy, People, Review.

Paul Docherty: You can sum the Hoshin process up in four words: Focus, Clarity, Alignment, and Follow-up.

1. **Focus**. Focus is about focusing only on a few key, wildly important goals, and success is as much about what you choose not to do than it is about what you actually choose to do. Without focusing, we set ourselves up from the beginning for failure.

2. **Clarity**. Clarity is about explicitly defining in terms everybody can understand exactly what success means. Clarity is not about saying we want to be the best space agency in the world. Clarity is about saying I want to put a man on the moon and bring him back alive by the end of the decade.

3. **Alignment**. Alignment is about getting as many people engaged with, as well as believing in, the particular plan you are trying to execute. Without a Hoshin-style cascade/catchball process to drive alignment, you can easily get what I call the 10-percent problem, i.e., less than 10 percent of employees' objectives are aligned with the goals (and even fewer can explain how their objectives support the goals),

which means that 90 percent of the energy of the organization is pointing in the wrong direction.

4. **Follow-up**. Follow-up is about relentlessly checking to understand whether your actions have actually moved the dial and then acting to do something about it if they are not.

THE HISTORY OF HOSHIN

Question to Lisa Boisvert: *You worked for Bob King back when Hoshin Kanri was very new in the United States. What has been lost from those early days that should be resurrected?*

Lisa: I ... think some organizations continue to apply Hoshin as part of an overall system of improvement, but it can also be seen as a stand-alone tool for planning now, outside a framework like GOAL/QPC's TQM Wheel.

In GOAL/QPC's Wheel, Daily Management, the starting point, is where each employee knows clearly and simply what he or she has to do in order for the organization to run smoothly. Next would come Vertical Alignment, which includes Hoshin Planning. Hoshin helps to align everyone around the direction of the company. And, then, possibly a more advanced stage of organizational development is Horizontal Alignment, where unnecessary organizational silos have been brought down, and the few core processes of the business can be managed cross-functionally.

Question to Bruce Sheridan: *You were involved in an early (maybe the first?) major application of Hoshin Kanri in the United States. Can you tell me about it, including how Hoshin Kanri became known initially as "Policy Deployment"?*

Bruce: Yes, I was there. I was at Florida Power & Light in the 1980s, and we had the Union of Japanese Scientists and Engineers coming to see us every three months, for about two weeks at a time. We were translating Hoshin Kanri into English, and it involved 16-hour days, with reviews continuing on Saturdays and Sundays. We all made a lot of mistakes. I believe one of the translation mistakes made at that time involved the name given to Hoshin Kanri by the Japanese—"Policy Deployment." Looking back, I believe it should have been translated as "Strategy Deployment." In the United States, "Policy" related more to Human Resource or Legal type of issues.

Question: *What prompted Florida Power & Light to take Hoshin Kanri on?*

Bruce: Our CEO at the time, Marshall McDonald, went to Kansai Electric in Japan on a benchmarking trip and saw a storyboard that showed meter reading errors. It was all in Japanese, so an interpreter was translating for the visitors. "As you can see, Kansai Electric is achieving its target of 20 missed meter readings." Reportedly, the CEO turned to another FP&L person on the trip and said, "What's the big deal? Our target at FP&L is 5." The interpreter went on with the explanation of the storyboard and said, "As you can see, they are significantly below the 20 missed meter readings *per million* meters read." The CEO refused to believe that this was possible. FP&L had a target of 5 missed readings per thousand and couldn't hit it, while Kansai Electric was achieving better than 20 per million? This meant that Kansai Electric's results were 250 times better than FP&Ls! With FP&L having 4 million customers, this meant that at best they had 20,000 meter reading errors per month, whereas Kansai Electric would have less than 80. The CEO came home, FP&L adopted Hoshin Kanri, and FP&L went on to be the first company outside of Japan to win the Deming Prize in 1989.

WHY USE HOSHIN?

Questions to Joe Colletti: *Why is Hoshin needed?*

Joe: I've found that American organizations are pretty good at figuring out what they need to do. The problem is with deployment—getting it done.

There are a lot of great consulting firms out there to help an organization figure out where they need to go and how they need to get there. The real question becomes: How do you get your plan deployed down into the organization so that everybody is aligned, both horizontally and vertically?

Question: *Your thoughts on how Hoshin impacts alignment?*

Joe: Here in the United States, we're pretty good at vertical deployment, but we're lousy at horizontal alignment. Hoshin gives you the ability to achieve both. If you don't know what someone on your left or right in the organization is doing, and you don't know that they're in trouble, how can you possibly help them?

Question to Larry Rubrich: *How do you know if an organization needs help with strategy deployment?*

Larry: A good test for effective strategy deployment involves asking the employees at all levels about the goals of the organization. When they don't know, or when they list a bunch of personal opinions, you know the organization's strategy deployment is ineffective.

Question to Jerome Hamilton: *What benefit did Hoshin Kanri provide at 3M?*

Jerome: Hoshin Kanri helped us to focus on the vital few priorities, the vital few objectives.

Also, within the 3M Industrial Business Group, the Kanri piece needed to be improved. We were really good at developing plans, but not so good at doing the check step all year to make sure our plans were being executed properly, and that we were getting the desired results by implementing them.

Question to Jeffrey Liker: *How are employee engagement and Hoshin Kanri related?*

Jeffrey: What I say in my books, and what I learned from Toyota, and what we practice is that "the only way to get employee engagement is to engage employees." You don't get employee engagement by talking about it, or by making managers more interpersonally sensitive. Employees must be engaged by leaders with a deep understanding of problem solving, who are teachers of daily improvement driven toward clearly defined targets. Once you have the improvement skills and a culture aligned around solving problems, you can connect the targets people work toward with Hoshin Kanri.

Question to Wes Waldo: *Why use Hoshin?*

Wes Waldo: The primary reason to use Hoshin is to directly involve the entire organization in fulfillment of the business strategy itself. It creates buy-in, and what I call an "emotional commitment" to the work to be done, not just a "fiduciary responsibility."

PREREQUISITES, CRITICAL SUCCESS FACTORS, SECRETS, AND KEYS TO SUCCESS?

Question to Wes Waldo: *One of your three words for Hoshin was "Stretch." Can you tell me more about that?*

Wes Waldo: The goal of Hoshin, from my perspective, is not meant to be merely project management. Some people devolve into that, and they use it as a tool to manage all of their activities. But, it's original intent was to create breakthrough objectives. It's not breakthrough if it's not stretching your organization. So, the goal is to pick something that you know you need to do, but you're not sure how you're going to do it.

Question: *What are the prerequisites for success with Hoshin?*

Mike Cowley: In my consulting work, I wouldn't consider helping a company unless I knew I had the support of the top management. It's really important to have the top leadership of a company engaged and convinced that something drastic has to change in the company, because Hoshin, for most companies, really is a dramatic change in approach.

The next thing would be that the education component is really pretty important. You need anecdotes, and it's really helpful to have people who have used Hoshin to come in and talk to the executives. We did that at Hewlett-Packard. We had people from the Japanese subsidiary, where we got a lot of insight from the experts before we launched into full-scale implementation of the process. And that helped. This was in the 1980s and there was a huge cultural abyss. The CEO at the time, John Young, really became convinced that we needed a change. He was smart enough to pick up a big business need that we had and put together a long-term vision for meeting that need. The basic need was to dramatically improve the quality of all of our products. A lot of people thought that HP products were the best in the world, and they were. But, compared to Japanese levels of expectation and quality of electronics, we were pretty low on the scale. And our Japanese customers told us that pretty bluntly. So, it's important to have leadership from the top so you can really get stuff done. You need to be able to get people's attention—call meetings and have people show up. The top guy's got to support it.

It's important to maintain a focus. There's a temptation for any process that seems efficient for getting a lot of stuff done. The temptation is to try to boil the ocean and apply it to everything at once, and that's a big mistake. You really have to maintain the focus. I always insist that clients select *one* Hoshin objective—maybe it's a six-month objective—and they put a full court press on that. Relegate everything else to ... "use the business practices we always did." Maybe you can make minor improvements, but make sure you focus on a legitimate business problem and make some progress in a six-month period. A lot of CEOs get greedy and want to solve their laundry list of favorite topics and problems, and that's a big mistake. It just overwhelms the organization.

Bob Dodge: You really need commitment and consistent visibility from the top; not just buy-in, and not just the launch, but regular reinforcement of the commitment and visible leadership. Without this, you are wasting time and money.

Barry Witcher: I would start on daily management/operations first. Get that sorted out before strategy deployment. Especially the PDCA principle.

David Silverstein: Make sure you have a REAL strategy, **not just clichés and buzz words**. Effective strategic planning is predicated on one big assumption ... that you have *a* strategy. Some have a vision statement, and a mission statement, and a bunch of buzz-words on the wall, but they don't have a ROBUST strategy.

Make sure you have a really good fundamental strategy before you start trying to use Hoshin to make a strategic plan. Do you really have a differentiating strategy and not just a bunch of things to do? That's what happens to most companies with Hoshin ... it becomes a "to-do" list, because they don't really tie back to a strategy. If they don't have a really well articulated strategy to focus on, then Hoshin just becomes a set of initiatives all over the map. *That's why it often gets called strategies—with an "s" (plural). A company should only have one strategy. If it's plural, there's something wrong.*

Greg Watson: If we take the perspective that the purpose of Hoshin Kanri is to steer organizationally strategic change management projects that have the support of the leadership team, then there are a couple of prerequisites that should help.

First, the organization needs a "predictive" type of performance measurement system. This is not a balanced scorecard. It is a system that allows the organization to use its internal process knowledge to predict future performance events based on factors that drive business performance results. This is different from financial measurement systems, which are based on average performance and a lot of guesswork. (We typically use the fancier term *allocation* in a discussion of the use of rules of thumb to make decisions in finance.)

Second, management must be committed to continual improvement. This implies that the senior business leaders accept their role as informed reviewers of performance improvement and that their decision-making contribution will be allowed to be steered by the variation that is observed in the process performance. Is this variation significant or is it just random noise?

Third, management will decide to choose improvement projects based on conditions of business change imperatives *and* process capability shortfalls.

And finally, business leaders must appoint competent process specialists to manage such change projects. Innovation, customer intimacy, and competence development are all required to steer the business organization in the future. What Hoshin Kanri does in this process is to improve the project selection and change management processes and increase the communications effectiveness throughout the formal and informal organization structure. This way everyone knows what strategic changes the management believes are necessary for the future health of the organization.

Question: *What are some important cultural factors for Hoshin Kanri readiness?*

Zane Ferry: [In answer to an earlier question] I alluded to what I firmly believe is the most essential requirement for strategic success by any organization—lasting commitment by company executives and directors to improve the life quality of every employee salaried and hourly. This is the ultimate strategic goal, which so few organizations attain. If we truly prioritize the development of employees by creating problem-solving skills, diverse functional competency, systems thinking, process-driven team-based responsibilities, self-awareness, and interpersonal communication skills, then our organizations become engines of strategic change driven by every interaction our people have with customers, products, their communities, and each other.

Narrowly speaking, a focus on people development is thought of by traditional strategists as an enabler for the real work of market positioning, acquisition, and product/service innovation. What research and standout success of certain companies have shown over the past 50 years is that creation of organization-wide effectiveness through intensive human resource development is the most successful long-term strategy. Methodically designing an environment where employees thrive physically, emotionally, and creatively attunes everyone to the key factors of their organization's success. "Nice to have or must have?" is the question I have to think Peter Drucker was responding to when he famously said to Mark Fields, then president of Ford Motor Company, "Culture eats strategy for breakfast."

Mark Caponigro: The ability to engage and maintain two-way communication is key. Hoshin Plans are not just posted on the wall by the cafeteria. Creating a dialog is important. There should be an effort to test for understanding and opportunities to educate. Deming's #1 was to have a constancy of purpose. The Hoshin Kanri process is a great vehicle to articulate the purpose.

Lisa Boisvert: Here are three:

First, *a compelling reason to change.* People either perceive that they're in crisis or that they're about to be. The crisis is often financial in nature. The more intense the anxiety, the more ready they are.

Second, an appreciation for *the correct pace* for the deployment. I've been involved with Hoshin Kanri for 18 years, and I've consulted in this space for 14. I still don't have a magic remedy for knowing the right pace up front. If an organization has already been through a large-scale deployment of a methodology, that often helps them have a better sense for the pace that will work best for them.

Third, there is a tremendous benefit to having *resident process improvement skills.* If the organization has some experience with mapping processes, conducting root cause analysis, reading run charts and histograms, that's a big help to a Hoshin deployment. It's not exactly cultural, but it's helpful for readiness.

Joe Colleti: Most organizations would find that Hoshin would work for them so long as leadership doesn't "beat people up" for what appears to be a lack of performance. One of the greatest things visibility does for you is that you can see where things are going wrong way ahead of time. A dysfunctional management practice involves "wading in and beating people up" when things aren't working instead of saying: "How can we help?" "How can we turn this around?" "What support do you need?"

As a leader, if you "beat people up" when things go bad, you will find that future datum gets obfuscated, it gets concealed because your employees are protecting themselves. For Hoshin to work, you have to have leadership that is committed to the success of the organization, meaning that you're going to help people succeed. And when you have that, it's really powerful.

Wes Waldo: The biggest critical success factor is that … you don't have to have the most senior leaders involved when you start this thing, but you cannot create a plan that runs counter to what the senior leadership vision is of the future. Some people will ask, "How can I get started if I don't have the CEO's involvement … it's just a waste of time." And I'll tell them, "No, it's not. It works very well at the business unit level in trying to get yourself organized and motivated. But if the plan you come up with at the business unit level, you show it to the CEO, and they say, "What are you doing? You're leading completely opposite of where we need to go," then you have a problem. So, even if you don't have the CEO involved, you still need to have an idea of their path and vision of the future.

Another critical success factor involves an organization's response failure. When you create a stretch goal, very often you're not going to quite meet it. And, what I run into a lot is companies will say, "Okay, we're going to grow revenue by 50 percent in two years." That's the Hoshin, let's say. And, they grow revenue by 45 percent. And, people look at that and say, "Well, we didn't succeed; we failed." And, I say, "Wait a minute. When is the last time you've grown revenue by 45 percent in two years?" And, their response is: "Well, never." It's critical to try to redefine what failure means in that environment.

Kevin Meyer: A desire to be aligned and focused on the future and an ability to willingly stop work on projects that do not align with the plan.

Steve Darrish: Hoshin Kanri must start from the mindset of changing the way the organization operates—the behaviors. In the perfect world, you want buy-in from the top. Build and get buy-off on the strategic plan at the enterprise level if possible, and begin to cascade the operating plans across the business units and down the functions. It is better to pilot the Hoshin Plan instead of trying to swallow the elephant in one bite. Ensure you are working in the impactful areas of the business if possible. Embed the plans using Kanri and drill objectives and targets into Human Resource mechanisms to ensure people are held accountable.

Do the math, do the metrics roll-up and drive the next level up performance; all the way to the strategic plan. If so, success.

Brian Leonard: For Hoshin Kanri, and Lean, in general, to be effective, there are numerous cultural obstacles we must overcome. Leaders must be willing to empower others in making decisions. Leaders often unfortunately believe empowering others means losing power, when, in fact, empowering others enables us to shift from managing to leading. The culture of power and control will prevent progress. Leaders must also be deeply involved in Lean, providing support and even participating in Lean initiatives in order to become well versed in Lean. Be visibly supportive, as noted by many Lean experts, and people will respond by taking ownership in project work. We must also seek to develop internal talent. When team members show genuine interest, then talent leaders should take every step to allow and encourage their development.

Executive leaders must also be willing to mandate Lean and to stick to that decision regardless of resistance. Communicate this mandate, then immediately reassure people their input is not only needed but critical. This mandate will often be met with negativity from department-level managers. This obstacle may very well be the toughest to overcome. Do all we can to get managers onboard, but do not turn a blind eye if managers become the anchor, preventing progress. Work closely with managers to educate them as to the basics of Lean, and get them involved early in supporting improvement initiatives, serving as process owners [who are] held responsible for results. In settings such as healthcare, executive leaders may also need to improve relationships between themselves and clinical professionals. Physician and executive leadership relationships are, in some situations, quite strained. There will be little or no lasting improvement until these relationships are improved—working all as one team.

Hourly team members must also have a new set of expectations. Everyone should be expected to participate in project work. Of course, this comes in time as not everyone can be pulled from their daily routine to work on projects. We can, however, expect everyone to begin contributing ideas for improvement. When these ideas are submitted, do not allow Lean to become a recommendation program. Act on employee contributions. To establish a Lean culture, it must become routine for everyone on all levels in an organization. Use Hoshin Kanri to build structure and help team members see how their efforts contribute to organizational goals.

Lastly, culture will not change until we have established new habits, with Lean being the routine. One way to achieve this is to change the goals we set for managers. Departmental goals and managerial goals must be tied to Lean metrics. Furthermore, if hourly employee job performance is being evaluated, we must modify the evaluation process to include contributions to quality improvement and process improvement.

James Hinkle: The biggest cultural requirement for Hoshin Kanri is support. When we first started, we had the necessary support from management; we were encouraged to try new things and look at things differently. As new ideas came up, they were not "shot down," rather, they were tested. We continued to meet as a cross-functional team, and though it was a little rough at the start, dialog soon came, and we were able to knock down silos and foster a mentality of strategy, support, execution, and communication!

Bob Emiliani: Desire to do Hoshin Kanri well, rather than half-assed.

Question: *What are the secrets to success?*

Mark DeLuzio: The key is focus on the critical few. The hardest thing to do with Hoshin is not figuring out what you are going to do … it's agreeing on what you are NOT going to do. Hoshin planning is all about focus!

Lisa Boisvert: There is a lot of subtlety to Hoshin Kanri. People who take an overly technical approach to it often fail.

Lois Gold: For an organization to do Hoshin really well, they have to be really grounded in process management, because all strategies are about figuring out which of your business processes are either broken or need to be created. Broken can mean literally broken or just maxed out in capacity. A strategy is just which process to fix, expand, or create. And to do that, you have to understand that the outcomes you're seeking are really driven by the processes that drive your business.

If a plan is about transformation, we know that fundamental to a transformation is process. You can only go so far by focusing on culture. You drive strategy deep into an organization because there are different levels of process granularity that have to be impacted in order to build back to your objectives and goals.

Let's say a corporation has an objective to increase market share in product X, and that's what they cascade down. Unless they create a decision tree and understand the cause and effect relationship among the processes that are going to get them there, along with the facts and data that determine "where are the holes?" Without all of that, you're just taking shots in the dark, and you're hypothesizing based on gut feel about what's going to improve your market share.

Mara Melum: Top leadership champions, first of all. Secondly, enough organizational pain that the company knows that incremental changes are not going to give it the success it wants. So, the company is looking for a breakthrough versus incremental change. Third, a good balance of wise judgment and use of the tools to make decisions. Fourth, developing a "golden thread" to ensure that the breakthrough goal really is deployed throughout the organization as opposed to just stopping after one or two levels. And fifth, continuous evaluation and improvement.

Question: *What are the Critical Success Factors for Hoshin?*

Lois Gold: The organization must be held accountable for resourcing and actually implementing the strategies. It doesn't matter what planning process you use. The senior management must really hold their direct report's feet to the fire, and so forth down the line as far as you need to go to cascade this to ensure that it is a priority of the organization. What happens is that a manager has many objectives, and they have some that contribute to the overall corporate goals, and they have others that contribute to their own functional goals, product line goals, etc. Unless the organization understands that you have to resource Hoshin goals first, and they hold people accountable by having strong metrics and a formal review process, it's not going to work. But, if you do that, you really drive accountability for the organization metric throughout the institution.

If you're doing this (Hoshin) well, you're looking at both your dependent and independent variables on a regular basis. So, you have transparency through a formal review process of "what's the deviation from plan?" And, if there is a deviation, how are you going to course correct it?

Essentially what you're doing when you put the plan in place is you're making a series of (hopefully) fact-based assumptions. "That if I do X, Y, and Z, ergo the strategy, that I will get the outcome that I'm looking for ... the objective and the goal." If your goal is moving in the right direction, but your strategy metrics aren't, then you don't know why you're getting your results. So, you may be fat, dumb, and happy, but you can't replicate it. And, you're at the whim of the same happenstance that drove you in the right direction could easily drive you in the wrong direction.

Hoshin also takes persistence. You have to start at the very top. Hoshin Kanri worked at HP [Hewlett Packard] for several years when we had a series of CEOs who understood it and held people accountable.

It takes patience and persistence. It's much easier to say, "… just give them a financial goal and let them figure out how to do it."

When you have multiline organizations and conglomerates, unless the organization truly develops shared goals, there is little incentive for the organization to work collaboratively.

People assume Hoshin is just a strategy planning device, but Hoshin doesn't take hold, and it won't be successful, unless it's part of a broader system that focuses on strategic metrics and is founded on strong process understanding and process metrics. So, people try to put it (Hoshin) in without that fundamental understanding, and the people that are asked to implement it and internalize it don't understand it. If you just brainstorm ideas, you don't drive a fact-based culture. In that kind of environment, you can do any kind of planning.

Mark DeLuzio: Hoshin needs to be process-focused and results-oriented. A lot of Strategy Deployment I see, people have 50 measures, and they'll deploy the measures. They'll say, "What is your department going to do to improve inventory turns?" What is

Manufacturing going to do? What is Quality going to do? What is Engineering going to do? You need to use cross-functional teams that work together on the same objective, but they work on the *process*. You need to deploy the process. You drive your action plans and your Kaizen activities toward building a better mousetrap that delivers results that are sustainable.

And, it all needs to start with a good strategic plan. If you don't have a good strategic planning process, you probably don't have a good strategic plan. Strategy deployment starts with a good strategic plan. And, regarding the strategic plan, I like to say, the quality of the plan is inversely related to the size of the book.

Your takeaway from the strategic plan is: "Here are my three breakthrough objectives." We developed two or three annual improvement plans (AIPs) per breakthrough objective. Many companies merely deploy operating metrics, which is wrong.

Question: *What advice would you give someone just starting out on their Hoshin Kanri journey?*

Beth Cudney: As with any journey, you must be flexible. As you start down this path, it is a new way of thinking strategically; therefore, plans will change as new challenges come to light. It is important to continuously communicate progress to all employees and provide appropriate training at all levels of the organization throughout the journey.

Gary Vance: I have two pieces of advice for someone just starting on their Hoshin Kanri journey. First, don't worry too much about the Hoshin Kanri planning format that you follow. There are many books, consultants, and plans available, and, for the most part, they are pretty much the same. The key is to select one and get started. You may have to make minor adjustments later, but that is better than spending months analyzing various options before finally making a selection. Second, don't underestimate the importance of the work that follows the initial planning. There are many examples of great plans gathering dust on a bookshelf. The planning is not always easy, but the follow-up is by far the hardest part requiring tremendous commitment and discipline. If you are not willing or able to commit to the follow-up, don't waste the time and money on elaborate planning.

Mark Caponigro: Understand the limitations of the process would be first. Assign someone to be "editor-in-chief" of the output. Inputs to setting the key themes come from conversations with multiple leaders. Generally, they do not speak the same way and will have different views on hot buttons. The editor will need to synthesize the input into a common language output that will be understood at the levels of the organization. The editor also needs to manage the cohesiveness of the language and intent through the layers of themes to goals to objectives to focus areas. The editor must also revisit the leadership to assure that the original intent is not lost or weakened by the modified wording.

Jane Dwyer: Don't make the mistake of cascading to all levels at the beginning, the task will be too daunting and there will not be enough commitment and understanding to drive buy-in and culture change. Ensure that the top level of leadership is committed and understand the value of the Hoshin process.

If the leadership says they want to engage all levels in the first year of Hoshin, then that is a sign that they do not understand what and how Hoshin works. Business and Culture strategy must align from the top first. Foundation must be set so that the next level can see the change in the status quo and see the commitment toward realizing our vision. There must be confidence and evidence of that before you engage the next level.

Rafeek Kottai: Communication is the key. You can never over communicate, so use all options possible. Consistent and timely communication must be maintained to gain trust and cooperation from all. Leadership must be actively involved in the process of setting goals and priorities.

LESSONS LEARNED?

Michael Cowley: I found in a lot of companies, upper management operated somewhat remotely from the rest of the employees, not really knowing what was going on. You're better off telling people what you're trying to do, and involving them as the Hoshin process is designed to do. Find something they can help with that is reasonably aligned with what you're doing for the breakthrough objective. My experience is that it makes work a lot better if you do that.

My personal approach has always been to be somewhat flexible in implementation; make sure that the really important elements are adhered to, but you are reasonably flexible in terms of format, that sort of thing. There are a couple of things that business groups are tempted to do, and one of them is to not do reviews. And, that's a big mistake. The review process is the most important, I think, of all of the steps. You learn the most from it. It's tempting to say, "These things are tedious and they take a lot of time" and "Let's just get on with it."

I also try to integrate the normal business planning, a lot of people call it a budget, but it's really a tactical plan, with the Hoshin plan for a couple of reasons. One reason is they compete for resources. And, the second is there's usually a huge amount of synergy between your normal tactical plan and the Hoshin, the breakthrough plan, in that you can kill a lot of birds with one stone in some cases. So, it's valuable to begin thinking about that, at least at the outset. If you do a good job of setting up what I describe as Daily Management—all the normal stuff you have to do to run the business and the business processes—if you set them up, over time with metrics and measures and goals and reviews, you begin to uncover things that are worthy of future breakthroughs. That happened in my division at HP when we found a business process that was not working too well. It was simply our manufacturing scheduling, where we scheduled the building of all of the products we sold. We had something like 1,000 line items that emanated from a few semiconductor processes, and we just didn't have a good way of scheduling those, all the way out to the point where we shipped to customers and committed to them to make a shipment in x weeks. And, it's very difficult to do that if you don't have a very robust scheduling system. So, one year, that's what we did. That was our Hoshin. And, it was remarkable. It enormously benefited the division. The customers were delighted, and the field sales guys were ecstatic, because we were able to pinpoint delivery times for product and meet our commitments.

My book is pretty detailed in the "nitty gritty" of getting ready for meetings. And that's important. You're bringing a lot of people into this thing and you owe them a well-designed process that someone has given thought to so that the meetings are efficient.

Lois Gold: Deployment of Hoshin can't be successful without a full Change Management Plan supporting it. Managers need to be trained in the concepts and methodology. You cannot just send out an email with templates and calendar and expect reasonable implementation. The notion of cascaded and linked objectives and strategies is not inherently obvious to people. If they don't understand the concepts, they will simply try and force the objectives they wanted to work on into the format, regardless of whether they truly support the top down objectives.

Tom Cluley: My experience with Hoshin Kanri is that nobody gets it right out of the chute. It takes several iterations.

Wes Waldo: You get people that get really excited up front, and you haven't properly prepared them for just how much work this is. People often look at it like it's some sort of "magic pill" they're going to swallow. But, when you're into your third or fourth month of your monthly review process and people are saying they don't have time, and they don't want to go to the meetings, or pull things together, you have to remind them that filling out the X-Matrix was the first and sometimes the easiest step. Sticking to the process year over year is the tough part. And to me, the lesson learned is making sure I have adequately prepared the entire team for just what the effort is going to look like.

Brian Leonard: Expect Hoshin Kanri to be extremely challenging for the first 12 to 18 months. The process of completing the Hoshin X-Matrix, in order to assess alignment between True North Metrics, Annual Objectives, Value Streams targeted for improvement, and proposed Lean projects, while seemingly common sense, can be highly stressful. One must be open to an entirely new way of thinking. Furthermore, possibly the best advice is to stick to it. Many abandon Hoshin Kanri claiming it is too difficult or of little value. The fact is simply this, if we are not practicing Hoshin Kanri to select projects, which will truly have an impact on the customer and our strategic goals, we are merely leaving it to chance. Regardless of how challenging it may initially be, we must stick to Hoshin Kanri and use it as our organizational GPS. Many also discover their strategic plan is poorly written once Hoshin Kanri is applied. If this is the case, use what you learn from Hoshin Kanri to help improve the way your strategic plan is written, enabling one to develop a strategic plan that is actually meaningful.

Barry Witcher: It's all about senior leadership. Leaders must understand and proactively manage the Hoshin Kanri process. It goes beyond implementation to seniors actually using PDCA [Plan-Do-Check-Adjust] to manage how people work. The way people do things revolves around how senior leaders do things. That's the basis of culture. In the United Kingdom, many of the Japanese firms took over sites and plants that had a long history of industrial trouble, and afterwards the Japanese seemed to instill new organizational cultures quite successfully. I don't really believe in culture. I believe in management. But, I do worry that human beings can't really manage (that's another story).

Question: *What is a major lesson learned?*

Jerome Hamilton: People need to understand the real purpose of the tools. Sometimes with Lean, people get "tool happy." For example, you can overdo A3s and you can overdo X-Matrices.

Question: *What are your words of advice with regards to using Hoshin Kanri?*

Ellen Domb: Prepare to do a lot of work. Hoshin sounds so sensible … you are going to establish strategies, and you are going to check the strategies for reality and how to achieve them, and then you're going to get everybody in the company understanding both the strategy and his or her personal role in achieving it. Then, as you and your team do your work, there's going to be a focus on how you do your everyday work so that it contributes to achieving the long-term strategy. This sounds incredibly simple, and management sometimes thinks that it means that once they get it set up and running, it's less work for them. Don't expect senior and middle management to do less work. You'll be doing more work. It's because you need to pay more attention. You need to realign constantly. You need to show people throughout the company by your actions, not just your words, that you really are committed to the strategy. So, the first thing I would tell you is *it's not going to get easier to manage under Hoshin.*

The second thing I would tell you is that the biggest change from conventional ways of management is the active review phase of Hoshin. In the first couple of years, you need to expect that you'll make a lot of changes as you go, and these changes have to be viewed as positive, in that, very often, when you start off, you have a five-year multiyear strategy, and you honestly don't know which are going to be the most important activities for creating it. So, you have to get started, but as you learn things, you can change the plan. And to me, that's the biggest difference between conventional MBO (Management by Objectives) and Hoshin. With the MBO approach, you make a plan and stick to it. With Hoshin, you make a plan and when you learn something, you might change it. *The power of Hoshin is the power of frequent review based on the "what did we learn and how do we change the plan to incorporate what we learned?" Hoshin is the only system I've seen that requires people to systematically go back and ask, "Are we doing the right thing?" … not once we've made the decision everybody runs with it.*

Question: *Speaking of a Hoshin focus, what are the dos and don'ts?*

Jim Buchanan: In my experience, Hoshin should be focused on the things that drive results, not on the results themselves. For example, I've seen organizations focus on financial results rather than the things that can drive those results, such as employee satisfaction and capability, and customer satisfaction. When you focus on the results, it's like trying to lose weight by stepping on the scale every day. You lose weight by focusing on the drivers of weight loss: diet and exercise.

Question: *Can you tell the reader about your Hoshin review meetings?*

Jane Dwyer: All levels are linked on their reviews through our Leadership Standard Work review meetings. As an example, Level 1 and 2 review a certain time every month, Level 2 and 3 do their review prior to this meeting, so that any issues, priorities, or misalignment get resolved or identified. If it is not resolved on this meeting, the Level 2 leadership will bring it up to the Level 1 meeting to resolve or reprioritize. Another meeting is set to flow down information from the Level 1 meeting and any adjustment that must be done.

This is done as a standard leadership cadence for us and is set on our yearly calendar. Metrics and actions from each level are reviewed during these meetings.

Mark DeLuzio: When Hoshin was first used at Danaher [Corporation], we allowed people to come in and explain away their problems. There were no countermeasures, no real problem solving. In our early Policy Deployment reviews, people would come with 40-page PowerPoint® decks and just "explain away." Policy Deployment should be centered around the Deming cycle: Plan-Do-Check-Act. We used Plan-Do-Check-Explain.

What to bring to the meeting? Four pieces of paper: an X-Matrix, a Bowling Chart, an A3 Countermeasures sheet, and an Action Plan. No PowerPoint. If you can't explain it using those four pieces of paper, you have to go back to the drawing board; 15 to 20 minutes per team.

Question: *What is management's role at the review meetings?*

Mark DeLuzio: It's not management's job to solve the problem for the team. A lot of VPs, in particular, think that they're the smartest people in the room, and they're going to solve the problem for the team. Their job is to make sure they've clearly articulated the problem, they're meeting frequently enough on their action plans to make meaningful differences, the countermeasures make sense. They're not there to solve the team's problem.

So many meetings I've seen go on for eight hours, because you've got all these big-headed vice presidents sitting saying, "I think you should do X, and I think you should do Y," and they don't have a clue what the problem is. A Toyota guideline: If the leader hasn't seen the problem and personally experienced it with his/her own eyes, he/she can't comment on it. How many times have you seen executives give their "two cents" on a problem when they have no clue what the problem really is? And that's when you start getting into real minutia. An organization that does well with Hoshin has the discipline to stay with the facts and stay with the data and not opinions or speculation.

Bob Dodge: Management has an opportunity to coach and mentor, which lessens the dependency on Management to have the answers. The keys here are asking questions and walking the talk.

Question: *How was the deployment at Danaher different from Hoshin Kanri at Toyota?*

Mark DeLuzio: Some companies are trying to be like Toyota, with regard to Lean and strategy deployment (Hoshin Kanri). This is a mistake. I think they need to be *Toyota-like*.

Question: *What advice would you give someone just starting out on his or her Hoshin Kanri journey?*

Zane Ferry: Some of my initial suggestions would be around clarifying expectations for the "journey" and better defining the "vehicle" for the trip. Start with the second part: ditch the Japanese term *Hoshin Kanri*. It's unnecessary. There are several good expressions for this in English. In my experience, jargon and foreign words do more harm than good in aligning diverse individuals to a common cause. Unless unique terminology generates itself naturally as a group matures and defines itself, it distracts and confuses. This approach to strategic execution will be challenging enough without foreign terms and secret handshakes at the door.

Next, what expectations do you have for this strategy definition and management process? Specifically, *what problems are you trying to solve?* This is the place to start. And it usually takes more time (much more time), thought, and analysis to answer that question than most organizations have devoted prior to rolling out new strategy initiatives. Charles Kettering's familiar quote, "A problem well-stated is a problem half solved," implies success depends upon good analysis. I've never heard anyone deny that out loud. Still, organizations that value their successful public image more than the need to learn and adapt (which is most) resist the notion they may not fully understand their true problems.

In most cases I suggest starting here, *before* the beginning of what most companies want to start doing when strategy creation and execution is their agenda. "We may not know everything, but we certainly know what our problems are," is a common unspoken reaction I see. Do not ignore it. Openness (or resistance) to reexamination of deeply imbedded organizational problems is the first test of readiness for adoption of the Hoshin Kanri process in my experience. At this point, you're still gauging maturity and organizational effectiveness. Remember, as you said in the question, this is a journey not a one-day trip to the beach and back. The metaphor of a journey implies that resources, endurance, cooperation, and adversity will all be challenges along the way. The group, whether it's an executive leadership team or goal deployment steering committee, will have to navigate these obstacles and establish numerous "base camps" as they advance. Assessing readiness, then shoring up gaps and establishing consensus about core organizational problems, is akin to testing the ground before pitching a tent or building a shelter. If the ground is soggy, uneven, or overly rocky, time will be wasted trying to get the tent stakes to hold. A sense of early failure may set in among stakeholders still tentatively onboard. So, avoid this with a systematic organizational culture and effectiveness assessment that combines thorough stakeholder analysis. A number of reliable models for this exist and I strongly suggest employing one or more of them to the fullest as preparation for Hoshin Kanri implementation.

Jonathan Ngin:

1. Be prepared to answer the difference between Hoshin Kanri and Goal Flowdown from leadership.
   a. The difference is Hoshin Kanri connects all levels of leadership via the X-Matrix, ensuring the organization's Top 3–5 "Breakthrough" Strategies are aligned to resources, who are assigned "SMART" projects that are tracked via A3 methodology.
   b. Goal Flowdown typically connects different levels of organizations via metrics that are designed to hit an Annual Operating Plan for Safety, Quality, Delivery, Inventory, and Cost/Productivity. Those metrics are then broken down by each level of leadership, where

employees are asked to come up with projects that will allow that team to hit their targets for performance.

2. Be prepared to explain that a Leader, who assigns an A3 that is tied to a "Breakthrough Strategy," also requires them to be a mentor, guiding the mentee through the journey of Discovery, Analysis, Change, Refinement, and Implementation. There are no shortcuts. Each phase must be well understood before moving to the next.

David Thomas: Hoshin Kanri is the first step on the journey to the successful implementation of a change program or a new project. Without it, the implementation may take a lot of effort, utilize (unnecessarily) resources, and may not be sustainable, so it must be done right [the] first time. Particular attention should be paid to receiving world-class coaching, mentoring, and skills transfer, especially in the technique of "*nemawashi*" (the achievement of genuine consensus).

John Petrolini: The establishment and implementation of Hoshin Kanri should be seen as a multiple-year journey not a short-term program. It is not for the faint of heart or the impatient. I would suggest breaking this highly integrated and complex system into multiple, manageable-sized pieces. For instance, the process of determining an overarching Hoshin Goal and/or identifying the vital few goals is significantly different than the challenge of deploying and communication goals throughout the organization, which is again much different than the challenge of learning to actually monitor progress and make midcourse corrections. In addition to this, there should already be a culture of problem solving (via fact-based gap identification and causal analysis) versus a typical culture of "let's brainstorm solutions to a particular problem." Finally, the first and most important requirement is that this is driven from the top of the organization, i.e., the CEO. The responsibility for implementation might be delegated to a senior individual, but the overseeing and management of it starts at the top. Without the involvement—not the interest, but involvement—of the CEO, the initiative will surely fail.

Judith Oja-Gillam: Those starting out on their journey need to ensure their sponsorship is sustainable for at least two years to be able to demonstrate positive results to strategic business outcomes.

Mark McDonald: Stay focused on effectively managing efforts to deploy a strategy for specific results; do not be distracted by details of tools and techniques that can be refined over time.

Kevin Meyer: Focus first on determining the key principles that govern your organization. Vision and mission may also be appropriate, but understanding and truly believing in the core principles is critical. From this, you can begin to look at long-term strategies, perform SWOT [strengths, weaknesses, opportunities, and threats]/etc. analyses to develop intermediate strategies, and then align the organization.

Steve Darrish: Advice—Start small, have early success, and expand on it. Ensure you have champions that can evangelize the approach. It doesn't have to start at the top, although that would be desirable. Hoshin Planning without performance measurement is not really Hoshin Planning. Make measuring easy to do. Pick a measurement approach where you can leverage existing systems if possible.

James Hinkle: Stick with it. When we first started our journey, it was tough. We struggled to figure out what we wanted to report and how we wanted to report it. We started off small, and bit-by-bit change occurred, and the process got better. To this day, we are continually monitoring what we are reporting and making changes as needed. We are still learning throughout the process; the important part is to stick with it.

Rafeek Kottai: You need to use the Hoshin review meetings to recognize and celebrate your wins, and never use Hoshin Kanri meetings to find faults or punish people. Even small wins need to be recognized and celebrated to create the momentum. All involved need to feel they are respected and provided opportunity (responsible freedom) to contribute outside of normal day-to-day operations.

Bob Emiliani: It takes three to four annual cycles before you really start to understand it.

Jim Bossert: Anyone starting out on their Hoshin Kanri journey needs to recognize that this takes two to four years to get the culture changed. It gets easier the more you do it. The first year is rough, and the plans are not as refined as they should be, but it is a start. It gets easier the second year and in the third year. My experience has been that the company then starts producing solid plans that are being cascaded deep within the organization. To expect change and excellence sooner is unrealistic. It takes time and you should plan for it.

Question: *What happens when an organization tries Hoshin Kanri before it is ready?*

Gerhard Plenert: Hoshin is a very powerful tool, and sometimes it's too powerful. It has to be put into the right organization, and it's usually an organization that has already developed some level of sophistication in its strategic planning. It's not for the organization that is just now trying to figure out how to spell "strategy."

Question: *What happens when a less sophisticated company (in terms of strategic planning) tries to use Hoshin?*

Gerhard Plenert: I'm talking out of experience here. It tends to scare them a little bit, because it is a little bit complex.

Unfortunately, I've worked with organizations like this, that don't know how to get together in a group, and know what strategy, brainstorming, visioning, goal setting is, if they've never done that before, and you come in there and whip out this Hoshin net for them, it's going to rattle them a little bit. So, you've got to work them into it a little bit. You've got to do a little bit of visioning: Where do you plan to be five years from now? And what is it going to take to get there? That kind of stuff. And then, once they've started understanding, these are the things I need to accomplish, and these are the steps it's going to take, and these are the people that are going to be involved in the accomplishment, then you can map it and say, "Look what we've got here; look what we've come up with." But, you've got to build them into it; you can't just come out and build a map and say, "Hey, guys, this is what we're going to do today." Ultimately, Hoshin is definitely the right long-term tool. If the organization is on track to make a difference, to get things accomplished, Hoshin is definitely the best tool.

If you take Hoshin and go into it one step at a time, using those same basic principles, it's the right way to go.

Question: *How should Hoshin plans be created?*

David Silverstein: If you're the boss, it's not okay to say, "I need a Hoshin plan for your department." If I, as the boss, don't make the time to sit down with my managers and develop that Hoshin plan with them so I know what's going on in their Hoshin plan, that it's rolling back up to support the overall corporate objectives, then shame on me. If I just delegate to my managers the creation of Hoshin plans for their department, because I've got to deliver that to my boss, then we've got a problem. It is my job to become their facilitator and to sit down with them and to actually do it together, to make sure it all ties together. And, too often people get too busy, and they delegate that, and that's why Hoshin breaks down and why it becomes a worthless exercise.

Bob Dodge: What David [Silverstein] says is true. At the same time, the boss should not attempt to develop it without the engagement and contributions of the team: the people with the perspectives, the people who will need to execute, and the people who will be impacted by the end result.

WHAT CAN GO WRONG?

Question: *Why doesn't Hoshin Kanri work in every organization that introduces it?*

Jeanenne LaMarsh: Because it is a change in how the organization plans and executes its strategy. And, that change often misses a key element that a change requires; namely paying attention to why people would resist that change. Here are some of the reasons:
- They don't see the need. Think the way things work today is fine.
- They don't understand Hoshin Kanri or don't like it; want a different process.
- The time it takes to do it takes time away from more important things like production.
- There are other changes in the organization that need their attention.

- The change effort to learn Hoshin Kanri is insufficient.
- They are not being held accountable for maintaining the discipline of following the process. There is no consequence for dropping out of that discipline.
- They do not see their management serious about, demonstrating their belief in, and enforcing this methodology.

And, there are more reasons that block the embracing of this as a change that takes at least a full-year cycle or more time of applying solid change management and project management until practicing Hoshin Kanri becomes the way the organization does its strategy design and execution.

Question: *Why does Hoshin Kanri fail?*

Larry Rubrich: There are success stories out there, but I will tell you there are many more failure stories. Primarily, failure with Hoshin Kanri comes from the fact that most leaders see Lean as a set of tools. Leadership might decide to "do Lean," but their definition of "doing Lean" is to find a Lean champion or a Lean facilitator and then hand the Lean implementation over to them. This is a mistake, because the greatest change in an organization, for Lean to be successful, occurs at the leadership level.

The leadership teams in most companies are used to telling people what to do and not taking the personal responsibility for doing it, for modeling it. They expect Lean to be some kind of "silver bullet" or "magic pill." They seem to believe that once they teach their people about Lean, it will just all magically happen. Leadership teams aren't prepared to do the hard work to get the whole thing started.

Question: *What can go wrong with Hoshin?*

David Silverstein: Hoshin can become merely a "to-do" list if it doesn't tie **deeply** to **core** or **fundamental** strategy.

Lois Gold: If you don't have the data to drive the strategies in the first place, so that your assumptions are fact-based, it can go very wrong. You can drive the wrong set of objectives and metrics.

Tom Jackson: They've built no linkage to the front line. If you get an MBA today, even from MIT, Harvard, or wherever, you're probably still learning. ... There are a couple of models of leadership that are still very dominant, even though we hear a lot of talking about servant leadership; really, people still grow up learning the command and control model of the Prussian military. And, then, on top of that, we add the old idea of management accounting of targets and audits that came out of General Motors. These are the constructs that I find most managers still live within. Many of them are still very "command and control" and those that have learned the General Motors system, the management accounting system of targets and audits, it's still very far removed. You learn about the disconnect between strategy and implementation far too late, and these are the failure modes. In the case of command and control, you literally disempower your workforce by telling them what to do. And, in the case of the General Motors' management accounting construct, the target and audit construct, it can be empowering, but not for enough people, and the feedback mechanisms are very sluggish. This is really why, in my mind, General Motors went bankrupt. Very sluggish feedback mechanisms, and they weren't really trying to implement Hoshin; they're probably thinking about it now.

Mara Melum: Common challenges include: (1) prioritizing many good ideas to come up with just one breakthrough goal; (2) shifting leaders' focus; and (3) seeing Hoshin as a bunch of tools instead of as a leadership system. And then you have the millions of things that can go wrong with people and people interactions.

Lisa Boisvert: Common mistakes made?

1. Choosing too many Hoshins.
2. Ignoring the organization's fear or resistance to change and undervaluing the need to lead the culture and communicate.
3. Not being clear about how success will be measured. A resistance to measurement in general.

Jim Buchanan: A company can start out focused on the "critical few," and then employees, customers, and shareholders start to add to the list, and you end up with the "trivial many." They lose focus. It definitely impacts the effectiveness of the Hoshin approach.

Wes Waldo: The thing that kills Hoshin is when you have too many objectives. To me, Hoshin is meant to be more of a deselection process instead of a selection process. Everybody looks at "how am I going to populate it?" I've never had a problem finding new opportunities. Our problem is always taking the list and narrowing the 20 down to the 8 or 9 that you need to do. Having too many objectives is that thing that usually goes wrong. Even if you're successful at getting people to understand that they can't have too many (objectives) in their top level matrix, people try to sneak in what I call a "bigger, higher-level objective," and they try to sneak them in somewhere down in the cascade. In other words, they will put their own objective down in a level 2 or level 3, that doesn't really fit, but they just couldn't let go of it. And, they say, "What's the harm?" Well, if everybody does that, pretty soon you're right back to where you started—too many objectives.

Gerhard Plenert: Implementation and execution problems occur because Hoshin assumes the organization already has an existing level of sophistication. For example, it assumes daily controls and performance measures are in place. If the information foundation exists, Hoshin is the most effective strategy planning tool at systematizing the strategic planning process.

Question: *What are some of the mistakes you have seen people make with Lean and Hoshin?*

Mark DeLuzio: The implementation of Lean can become the objective, Lean can become the strategy. And, that's the wrong objective, the wrong strategy. I believe your strategy is your business strategy, and it's customer focused, and it takes into account all your stakeholders. You then need to align your Lean initiatives, your Kaizen activities, with your strategy.

Question: *Why aren't more companies using Hoshin Kanri?*

Ellen Domb: Because it's hard work. It's so much easier to go on a three-day retreat, set up the plan, and then spend the next year meeting your quotas. Frankly, I'm not surprised that more companies are not using Hoshin for strategic planning. As a public company CEO, you hear the following about Hoshin: First, I have to spend a lot more time. Second, everybody in my company is going to be critiquing the plan. Third, strategic planning is not going to be a "once a year thing," it's now going to be a monthly and quarterly reexamination of the plan, including changes to the plan when we find out we're doing dumb [expletive deleted]. And, then, I have to go off and explain quarterly changes to the board of directors. I'm going to look like a "wishy washy" nonleader, because other people are telling me what to do. So, from a classical CEO's point of view, I can see Hoshin as being a very hard sell.

Question: *What are the biggest obstacles to Hoshin?*

Jeffrey Liker: The biggest pitfall in using Hoshin Kanri is when you don't have problem-solving skills, and you don't understand Lean methods.

Question: *What are the biggest mistakes made by those using Hoshin?*

Paul Docherty: The first thing that causes failure in an organization that attempts to introduce the Hoshin process is overconfidence, i.e., not recognizing that defining and cascading goals using a Catchball process is hard, and that it takes effort and needs facilitation, particularly when the management team involved is not used to a more structured approach to causal thinking. My advice is to ensure you bring in some external facilitation support for the early sessions; somebody who has real experience of how it works in practice and can guide the team to apply the process in a systematic and disciplined way.

The second reason why Hoshin fails is that it tends to be an activity where there's a lot of energy and excitement in the initial cascade process and only a fraction of the energy and excitement in the part that really matters—the ongoing execution and follow-up. Successful organizations focus on creating an execution "heartbeat" by establishing a monthly timetable of reviews (often called the Monthly Operating Reviews, or MOR, process). These reviews keep the team focused on the goals by forcing a regular assessment of not just whether the teams are on track, but what is being done to ensure they stay on track.

Probably the third biggest mistake (and this is in my experience the thing that leads to failure in the longer term) is not creating the kind of supportive leadership culture needed to make Hoshin stick. I think the fundamental problem is that, in many organizational cultures, the default behavior (when, for example, they see a red traffic light on a chart) is to blame people for things not happening, rather than seeing it as a signal of a problem in the future that they, as a leadership team, have an opportunity to resolve. Building a leadership culture that is open to bad news, focuses on support rather than blaming the team, and values the perspective of the team on what can be done and how it should be done is most likely to be able to succeed with the Hoshin approach.

There are many other practical, obvious ways you can make mistakes, but in terms of really wasting the energy, those are what I would say would be the big three.

WHO USES HOSHIN KANRI?
(AND WHY NOT MORE USERS?)

Question: *When/where have you see Hoshin Kanri used with success?*

Ellen Domb: Hoshin seems to work best when it fits the CEO's personality. In my experience, even a board member can't bring Hoshin into a company. It needs to be "personally owned" by the CEO. And, this won't help you being a business unit president within a billion-dollar corporation, but it seems to work well in small- to medium-sized companies where ownership and decision making are one.

Question: *Who, in your opinion, is using Hoshin Kanri most successfully?*

Michael Bremer: I've observed that very few companies are using Hoshin to great benefit: Danaher and Autoliv to name two. And, the most successful organizations have been influenced by Toyota, but they're walking a different path.

Question: Why aren't more companies using Hoshin?

Mara Melum: It can appear overwhelming. Many companies are looking for a streamlined approach. Many organizations are doing parts of Hoshin, they just don't call it that. I wouldn't say it's not catching on.

When I talk with organizations, they are often looking for a Hoshin-type transformation with a breakthrough goal. And most companies I work with want to harness and engage the power of their people ... which gets back to Hoshin processes like catch ball and alignment. Many elements of Hoshin are part of organizational leadership systems.

DIFFERENT APPROACHES TO HOSHIN?

Question: *Have you seen different approaches to Hoshin?*

Joe Colletti: Every organization I've worked with over the years seems to do it a different way. Given a standard Hoshin deployment chart, they will modify it to fit what works for them. They make it their own. This is also true of the Japanese companies I studied.

With a few forms of Hoshin Kanri implementation I've seen, the organization spends more time updating complex charts than achieving the plan itself. I believe it's best to start with a simple approach and then grow from there.

Question to Mark DeLuzio: *What was different about the Hoshin Kanri deployment you led at Danaher?*

Mark DeLuzio: There are several flavors of Hoshin out there in the marketplace. Most are very operationally focused. The Hoshin that I developed for Danaher in the early 90s (and they are still using it today) is more strategic- and business-oriented, focusing on strategic breakthrough objectives, not strictly operationally focused. Most Hoshin deployments I've seen are strictly an Operational play, focused on Quality, Delivery, and Cost, and Operational metrics. The Hoshin deployment at Danaher was about implementing our strategy.

Question: *What types of Hoshin Kanri have you seen? Can you explain this?*

Michael Bremer: I believe there are two basic "flavors" of Hoshin Kanri, and most organizations are using what I will call "Type I." Type I is about the Current State. It's based on where we are right now as an organization, and the question being asked is: "What are the right things to do?" Then there is what I will call "Type II Hoshin Kanri." Type II is about the Future State, and the question is: "Where do we need to be as an organization in x years?"

Question to Michael Cowley: *What departures did you (at HP) make from the Japanese Hoshin Kanri approach?*

Michael Crowley: When I went to Japan in the 1980s, what I found was that most Japanese companies were not using Hoshin. And, many didn't know what we were talking about when we said, "What about Total Quality Management?" That changed over time. What we did find was that the Japanese had many different styles of using Hoshin, so it's really hard to nail down one Japanese style. I was baffled by a lot of the literature that I read 15 years ago when we wrote the book. Because there were so many different Japanese experts, all had a somewhat different approach to Hoshin. So, it's hard to answer your question. We adopted pretty much of the methodology at Yokagawa that Hewlett-Packard was using.

IMPORTANCE OF VISION?

Question: *What is the importance of Vision?*

Michael Cowley: Doing the Vision properly really, really makes a difference, because it's a good point of departure for setting objectives. A lot of executives just want to set objectives, yet doing all of the work that leads up to the Vision, including the Vision, creates the context for setting the objectives. A lot of times, the executives have complete 180 turnarounds when they decide what it is they really want to do after they go through the Radar Chart and the Relationship Diagraph; whatever you want to call it. If you want to call the ID the Cause and Effect diagram, that's fine. It is reasonably important and helpful to go through all of those steps, in particular, the Vision. In reality, you don't have to do all of the preparatory work to do a Vision, but I think you get a much better one if you do the preparatory work. Sometimes, with a small group, I'll just say, "Let's create the Vision, and imagine out two or three years, what do we want to be like?" That just opens up a lot of good ideas, and it calibrates all of the participants against each other as to where their thinking is. And, it's valuable to bring divergent thinking into the process. This is a way of doing it.

Lisa Boisvert: With most clients—after the usual front-end work of assessing the environment, SWOT analysis, etc.—we begin by painting a picture of an ideal state 3, 5, 10, 20 years out, depending on the pace of their industry, how they are owned, etc. Working backwards from that vision increases the odds that the priorities we choose today are the ones that will lead to where we want to go.

The Affinity Diagram is a strong tool for building that vision as a group. The Interrelationship Digraph then helps the leadership team determine what parts of the vision are most likely to leverage the system toward the desired state.

HOSHIN OBJECTIVES: HOW MANY AND WHAT SHOULD THEY BE?

Question: *Hoshins? How many?*

David Silverstein: I believe that keeping things fairly simple with Hoshin is smart. I try to have a lot of discipline around the number of major Hoshins—five to seven maximum; three or four is okay.

Lisa Boisvert: One! Okay, maybe two, but maybe not. I've been working with executive teams on Hoshin Planning in different sized organizations and different industries, sometimes with lots of resources available, and very smart people since 1998, and I still believe that achieving one Hoshin at the *breakthrough level* is what most organizations can manage.

Could you achieve 10 to 20 percent success on several objectives concurrently? Probably. Can you knock more than one major organization-wide breakthrough improvement out of the park fully at one time, probably not. Hoshins are not incremental improvements.

Lois Gold: Big organizations can certainly benefit from Hoshin, but you can't drive more [than] one to three (maximum) Hoshin strategies or objectives through your organization.

When an organization has nine objectives, it shows a lack of understanding of prioritization and resource allocation. It doesn't matter what strategy planning process you use if you have that many objectives. The goal of Hoshin at HP? What are the critical few things that had to be done that year or during that multiyear planning cycle? And, the concept of the critical few got lost somewhere along the way. It will be just as unsuccessful in a monoline business if you don't understand that concept.

Question: *What should a Hoshin objective be?*

David Silverstein: Some clients want to include things like, "14 percent EBITDA [earnings before interest, taxes, depreciation, and amortization], because that's what I'm accountable for to my board." I tell them, "No. That's not a Hoshin. That can be one of our metrics."

Question: *What are your thoughts about Hoshin objectives?*

Paul Docherty: … when you think about the things that you're deploying, that you focus on the process that you're trying to influence. Let's take an example. If you say, "A Hoshin objective might be to bring a new product to market." Well fine, but the Hoshin objective should be about shortening the cycle time, or improving the efficacy of the process to bring a product, not a specific product being brought to market. And, I think a lot of times organizations focus on objectives which are one-off objectives rather than solving the process. That's where the real multiplier gains come from with Hoshin.

Wes Waldo: For the "South" in the highest level X-Matrix, I don't want it to be tactical in nature. I want it to be something that's bigger, more visionary, something that's really a stretch "go get" that you don't know how you're going to do it. It's almost impossible when you're doing this with a team to not come up with some sort of target around revenue or profitability, or both. Of the three to five breakthrough objectives, which is how many I recommend (most organizations have more than that), you're going to have one or two around financial. So, I tell them [that] once we get those in there, now we need to focus on the other parts of the business. What about your infrastructure? What about your learning and development? What about your customer that we need to create some sort of objective around? When we look all the way around the "North" in that X-Matrix, when I get to the Improvement Priority, I teach people to start off writing what I call "job to be done statements;" we pull this from the Innovation lexicon because very often what they do, if I take it more to the tactical level and a Kaizen event and you look at the problem statement, and what you're seeing is a solution. It's not about resolving the problem, but I want you to go implement this solution. I tell them, "You don't really need a problem-solving team for that. You need some engineers and a Gantt chart if you already know what you want to do." The same thing should be true for what's up "North" in the X-Matrix. It should be written more in the form of: "What is the job to be done," and then let the lower-level teams become more tactical and determine the best way to go make that happen. It's a bit of a learning point for most people because they don't get comfortable with writing their "job to be done statements" up front. I already know what I want to do. But, we find that's when you start to cut off things like new business model selection, some of the more innovative acquisition strategies if you're not careful.

CASCADING OF OBJECTIVES?

Question: *How many layers to cascade down?*

David Silverstein: I'd rather *err* on the side of a little too much than a little too little. Why? Because people get more done when they have goals and objectives. They just work a little harder, and they get a little bit more done. So, I err a little bit more toward driving it down that extra layer, risking it getting a little messed up as opposed to not having it, because it's kind of like sales. Sales is an activity-driven type of thing. The more calls you make, the more emails you send out, the more opportunities you're going to get and the more sales you close; even though you know some of that is wasteful effort, some of it is inefficient, some of it we're calling the wrong people. But the more activity, the more results we get. We know that. That tends to be true also as people tend to get hunkered down in their day-to-day job, and if they have that Hoshin plan, then there's something else in addition to their day-to-day job that they are getting done to help move things forward.

Question: *How do you know when you are ready to cascade to the next level?*

Jane Dwyer: When the current level can show understanding of the process and articulate benefits of the Hoshin process. This can be assessed by:

- All in the Current Level have a consistent understanding and [are] able to show how tools that we use work. (Example: Feedback from outside auditors, such as OSHA or ISO, telling us that interviews with top management reflects consistent understanding of our Hoshin process.)
- Those in the Current Level are able and willing to facilitate a Hoshin development process for their next level down.
- The Current Level wants and shows need to move to the next level as a group. (Feels confident that we are showing the correct values through actions that reflect our vision).

THE PDCA CYCLE (PLAN–DO–CHECK–ACT)

Question to Tom Jackson: *In your book,* Hoshin Kanri for the Lean Enterprise *[Productivity Press, 2006], the PDCA process is preceded by a "Scan" step. Can you please explain?*

Tom Jackson: Yes, a company should start by scanning the environment before they charter a team. This Scan step is intended to define a problem or a challenge for strategy to address.

Question to David Thomas: *You mentioned that some use PDSA versus PDCA, where "Study" is substituted for the "Check" step in PDCA. Can you please explain?*

David Thomas: Some experts have recommended that we change the word Check to Study. The reason, I understand, is a concern that the metrics being gathered were merely being ticked as collected, but not acted upon as such (check mark = a tick in the box). As long as the metrics existed, it did not matter whether they were good or bad or off target as long as they were collected. The desire is for them to be analyzed and the root cause identified and acted on, hence, changing the step to Study.

THE CATCHBALL PROCESS

Question: *What about Catchball?*

David Silverstein: Catchball is a good process. It's mostly about talking about the things we need to do and the obstacles we need to overcome to implement strategy.

Lois Gold: For Hoshin to be successful, you need the Catchball perspective, which is not command and control. It's got to be a top-down, bottoms-up, meet in the middle; really figure out what the right targets and things are. In a typical command and control environment, unless senior management's approach is fact-based, the targets they drive down into the organization are often just not doable.

Question for Jane Dwyer: *How does the Catchball process work at Knoll?*

Jane Dwyer: The Catchball process is ingrained in our Leadership Standard Work, which is our cadence on when we do our reviews and Hoshin development.

We start review and planning for the next year in September. We go over our Core Values, Vision, performance against our metrics and actions for the year, confirm relevance to our Vision, and define and prioritize gaps that must be resolved for the next year. Then, we start developing the Level 1 breakthrough objectives and strategic actions for the following year. (This is done with Level 1 and 2 leadership team.) Once agreed, the Level 2 is guided by the Level 1 Actions and start to develop their Level 2 actions with the help of their Level 3.

Once Level 2 Hoshin development is completed, we use the X-Matrix to check for alignment across all the areas. Any actions that are lacking supporting actions from another department between Level 1 and 2 must be discussed and realigned. Then, the next level does the same process. Alignment check is done between and across all levels during this process. Any misalignment is reviewed and resolved on our next monthly Hoshin review. If any actions or priorities change during the course of the year, all level X-Matrix actions will get adjusted.

Wes Waldo: To me, Catchball is one of the more enjoyable elements of this. The strategy process is often what I call a "go to the cave" mentality. What I mean by "go to the cave" [is] if you get the top 20 or 30 or 50 leaders, they'll go off for two or three days to some offsite session, and they will come back with something they will call "the strategy." And, the problem is that the goal is to try to get it rolled out by the end of the fiscal year, because January, everybody is supposed to start running with what their objectives are, but they spend the next month or two trying to defend it, explain it, get people to understand what they're talking about because they never got involved to begin with. So, they're spending all that time doing change management and communication when you're in March before most people get running on their objectives. And, this is a very common problem that we run into, and that happens when you "go to the cave."

The opposite of "going to the cave" is what we call Catchball. With Catchball, the goal is for those top-level leaders to start off with those breakthrough objectives. Once they have an idea of what those are, they quickly get down to the next level of management and say, "What do you think about this?" The next level of management might not be able to completely change it, but they should be able to influence it. And, they continue to do that as you move down the different levels of objectives—you're going back and forth. By the time we are done creating the strategic plan, everybody has already seen it. It's not a surprise.

There's not an unveiling that has to happen where some organizations treat strategy like an event. We had the offsite event; now we're going to have the communication event, and everybody going to go home for Christmas with their head spinning thinking, "What in the world just happened to us?" Whereas, what happens with Catchball is that everybody has their fingerprint on it and had some ownership and helped create the emotional commitment to this process. Now, they're not trying to defend somebody else's idea, they're defending their own, or at least something they had a chance to participate in. To me, that's the beauty of Catchball.

What people sometimes misunderstand with Catchball is that they expect all of the strategy to come from lower levels of the organization. It's quite the opposite.

Question: *How does change management fit into Hoshin Kanri?*

Wes Waldo: I've never been a huge fan of just saying, "Okay, we're going to do two days of training on change management and then everybody's going to be good to go." I think the only way to do change management is to build the tools and techniques right into your everyday process. So, for example, Catchball is meant to be the change management vehicle within Hoshin Planning. It's to give people the chance to make suggestions. The monthly review process itself is part of the change management vehicle, because if you have scorecards that people can see, they can see their efforts resulting in changes to the numbers, and they can see whether they're behind or ahead. Then, they can get a lot more excited about some of the work they're participating in. To me that's part of change management. So many times we wait until a quarterly review or a six-month review to let people know how they're doing, and they get surprised. And, then, all of a sudden they're playing catch up. To me, the way we set up Hoshin Planning itself, it's designed to have those change management techniques already built into it, if you do it right. But, if you skip out on the monthly reviews, and if you skip out on having people do their action plans and their A-3 reports like you're saving their time, the truth of it is you're cutting out the people part of the process and I think that's a mistake a lot of folks make.

Bob Dodge: Any time you attempt to implement a change in direction, approach, methods, tools, people, etc., if you don't identify who might resist, why they would resist, and mitigate that resistance, you might as well not start.

THE HOSHIN TOOLS

Question: *What are your comments regarding the value and use of the Hoshin tools?*

Lisa Boisvert: The tools do at least three things:
- Make the planning work visible
- Organize a large amount of discussion "data" into usable form
- Provide a process and mechanics that support executive teams in working well together.

AFFINITY DIAGRAMS

Question: *What are your thoughts regarding the Affinity Diagram?*

Michael Cowley: Another thing that I consider valuable, and it's fairly difficult to do, because I think American culture is that the really smart people work by themselves and come up with great ideas, patent them, and all that sort of thing. And the value of "group think" is underestimated. Personally, I'm a big believer, at least at the outset of some project, in getting all of the people that are going to be involved in a room together to do several things. One would be to create the vision of what this project is going to do for us, and how is it going to do it. Whether it be the strategic plan or a new product or a new business process and then again when the implementation starts, what are all the things we have to do? I personally find the Affinity Diagram a really helpful process. It gets people talking to each other. It gets an enormous amount of material on the table in a manageable form. So, if you do nothing else, I suggest you use Affinity Diagrams.

A client had an enormous project that was absorbing all of their energy. They wanted to buy up all of their distributors and they had no idea how to do that. I got the executives together, and we just did Affinity Diagrams, what are all of the things we have to do. And, within an afternoon, we had a pretty damned good plan of attack. The executives were amazed at how effective that was and how "on board" it got 25 or 30 people in the room. It was relatively smooth sailing; they pretty much put the plan together themselves, and the natural leaders emerged from the group. It was fairly amazing.

[The following is from Michael Cowley and Ellen Domb's book, *Beyond Strategic Vision: Effective Corporate Action with Hoshin Planning* (Routledge, 1997, pp. 170–172). With permission.]

Even at the Hoshin 101 level, if people knew how to do nothing else, I'd make sure they knew how to do the Affinity Diagram. If you're trying to put a plan together, for doing anything, I don't care what it is, as complex as you can imagine, this is a pretty good way to do it. At the strategic level you can use it to identify your strategies. Let's critically look at what we've created here, poke holes in it. Critique it. It's important to step back and perform a mathematical analysis and say, "Is this really going to work?"

I, a lot of the times, jump right into an Affinity Diagram with the executives, especially if there is some god-awful problem going on that needs to be fixed right away. The philosophy is that the house is burning down. We've got to put the fire out first. Yeah, we can do strategic planning and prevent future fires. So, we start right off, what are we going to do? At eight o'clock in the morning you do an Affinity Diagram. First, what do we have to do to fix our problem, and then, second, avoid a repetition, and then, third, find the root causes (PDCA), the standard problem-solving methods. A lot of times the answer is right in front of you if you ask the right people. I've found that time and again. And, it might emerge in days where it [otherwise] might take weeks or months if you run it through the normal chain of command. I consider that tool (Affinity Diagrams), if they learn nothing else, but they know how to use that tool, that's a valuable new skill.

THE X-MATRIX AND THE A3

Question: *There seems to be a lot of confusion about the use of the X-Matrix and the A3. Can you please help clarify things?*

Tom Cluley: Basically, the X-Matrix tracks the entire strategy deployment, linking the cascading structure from the Breakthrough Objectives to the Enterprise Annual Improvement Priorities down to the lower-level Annual Improvement Priorities, ensuring that there are tangible targets and that the efforts are resourced.

The A3s are narrower in focus, creating a disciplined PDCA approach to each supporting objective or project, following a process similar to DMAIC (Define, Measure, Analyze, Improve, and Control). The problem statement and various stages of the PDCA are posted on a single A3-sized document.

Gerhard Plenert: The X-Matrix is an overall strategy planning tool used for tracking strategic priorities and activities. It validates the cost/benefits, confirms that each project is sponsored and supported correctly, and ensures that the project has strategic alignment.

The A3 is focused on one specific project/activity/RIE and tracks "what we doing/why are we doing it/who has authorized it/what metrics will be used to govern it." The A3 then tracks the root cause analysis, creates solution countermeasures, and tracks the execution of the countermeasures. The A3 manages the specific steps that one specific project should go through in a lot more detail than the X-Matrix, and it standardizes that process for the entire company.

Bruce Sheridan: For the sake of discussing the X-Matrix and the A3, let's think of Hoshin Kanri in three major steps: Strategy Development, Organizational Alignment, and Execution. Using this setup, the X-Matrix is specifically targeted for Organizational Alignment and the A3 for Execution. Even though they are used at different stages, the X-Matrix and A3 share an attribute. They both serve to provide an organized view of a vast array of information arranged logically to communicate a message or a story that otherwise would be difficult to see. The X-Matrix links the Long-Term Strategy, Tactical Agenda, Projects, and Metrics all on one page in addition to discussing how the work will be resourced. The A3 is named for the size of the paper typically used to display the information, A3 or, in the United States, 11 × 17. The A3 is used to guide a project team through the execution of their work using predefined steps. During the project, the A3 serves to guide the team through problem solving or lean steps as well as serves as a way to update peers and management on progress. In the end, the A3 serves as a storyboard documenting the improvement achieved by a project team.

Tom Jackson: The A3 (referring to either Toyota's strategy A3 or its problem A3) is essentially a high-level project plan. You can also view it as a team charter.

An X-Matrix is a table of A3s. Normally these are strategy A3s, but can incorporate problem A3s as they crop up during the course of the year. The X-Matrix is used to check the alignment of multiple A3s by analyzing them in different dimensions. The dimensions I include in my X-Matrices include:

1. Thematic, i.e., does the A3 in question contribute to high-level strategic themes or goals? These themes or goals are normally recorded to the west of the X.

2. Financial, i.e., does the A3 in question contribute the bottom line? I park financial targets south of the X.

3. Process-related, i.e., does the A3 in question contribute significantly to leading indicators of financial success? The [key performance] indicators (KPIs) often appear to the east of the X.

4. Resource-related, i.e., what human resources are required to execute? The human resources appear to the far east of the X.

Sometimes, it is helpful to write a master A3 that corresponds to the X-Matrix. This helps leadership boil down its elevator speech to its essentials. I have also drafted A3s to define strategic themes (and define KPIs). But, the main interpretation of "A3" will be the first one I listed above, namely, either strategy or problem A3s.

Question: *What is the secret to success with the A3?*

Tom Jackson: It's not about the A3, it's about the coaching relationship between the manager and the supervisor or the CEO and the vice president. Hoshin really is a structure of coaching "dyads" (two people working together) … "coaching duos" might be a better way to explain it ... and to establish that relationship takes time. It took Toyota 10 years to do Hoshin from the board-room at NUMMI and down to the frontline supervisor level. So, I think that's plain ol' Toyota conservatism. I don't think you need to take 10 years, but that shows you how careful they were. And so, when you're first getting started, I like to say (and I think this is particularly true of small companies), keep the circle of involvement; define the circle of involvement, and keep it. Start off small, and then grow intelligently.

THE HANSEI–HOSHIN REFLECTION TOOL

Question: *Can you please explain the origin of the Hansei–Hoshin Reflection tool? Where did it come from? How/when do you use it?*

Jane Dwyer: We do Hansei every quarter as part of our Leadership Standard Work, to allow us to reflect and do a strategic PDCA process. This process allows us to review where we are and to see if we need to make any adjustments on actions, focus, and priorities.

The Hoshin reflection tools that we used were created from a series of information that I researched from several sources: Lean article, Hoshin process Internet search, and Lean Culture book. We picked the tools that apply best to our group and use it as an evaluation of our maturity. It's also tied into the Leadership Training that we designed specifically to support the Hoshin process.

METRICS

Question: *What about metrics?*

Jim Buchanan: Let's use customer satisfaction as an example. You need to really think through the logic tree—the cause and effect—and then identify the drivers of customer satisfaction and how best to monitor and measure it.

Bob Dodge: Remember, if you can't measure it, you can't manage it. This is a very tough concept for many.

BALANCED SCORECARD VERSUS HOSHIN?

Question: *Many organizations use the Balanced Scorecard. Is it the same as Hoshin Kanri?*

Joe Colletti: The question I would ask a Balanced Scorecard user is, "How are you deploying your Scorecard down into the organization? What is your process, your visual process, for deploying the strategies required to achieve the key metrics down?" Nine times out of 10, I'll bet you that information is not available to the people who need it. It's written down in a book somewhere, and it's on somebody's desk. Also, the Balanced Scorecard tells you *what* you've ultimately got to accomplish, it doesn't tell you *how* you're going to achieve it.

Wes Waldo: When I teach it, I don't teach it as one or the other, but I do think that both have a "home." One of the biggest problems people have with Hoshin Planning is that they see that as the actual strategy creation. You have to figure out where the original breakthrough objectives come from. What are those things that go into "South" of whatever the top-level matrix is going to be? To me, the Balanced Scorecard is an efficient and effective tool to help make sure we have looked at the breadth of objectives that should be out there. And, looking at those four different perspectives and saying, "Am I over-representing financial?" "Do I have something from infrastructure?" "Do I have something about people?" It forces me to look at the total breadth of objectives that need to be out there. So, I use the Balanced Scorecard to help me populate the top-level matrix. Then, the more effective of the two tools for doing the cascade and actually communicating it down into the organization and coming up with the tactical plan; that's when the X-Matrix really takes over, and it's much more effective, and the Hoshin Planning process works much better. I've had people use the Balance Scorecard, and they feel like every level of the cascade has to have one of each of the metrics. They had to have four, one for each of the quadrants. That's not the case. You get down to an engineering department, and they may not have anything in particular to do with "HR-type" objectives.

Question: *What are the pros and cons of the Balanced Scorecard versus Hoshin?*

Tom Jackson: There's a lot to like about the Balanced Scorecard. The thing they got right was you can't get where you want to go without managing the methods and means by which you intend to achieve your targets, and that's one of the things the Balanced Scorecard does. I often use the Balanced Scorecard literature. My background is in economics, and I taught business for years and years, so there's really nice literature that I can dip into and give the kind of theoretical foundation.

What the Balanced Scorecard did *not* get right is they really didn't see a true purpose, at least in my perspective. The Balanced Scorecard tends to live in the boardroom. I've rarely seen companies that have managed to link their Balanced Scorecard with frontline operations. And, so, there's a lot of talk, there's a lot of spending on fancy consultants (like me); you have a lot of beautiful charts, but there's really not a lot on the bottom line that I've seen. It doesn't get connected to operations. Where Hoshin excels, if you understand it correctly, is that you don't stop. You don't stop deploying until you make that final linkage between strategy and what happens at the front line of operations. I often tell the clients, "I will know when you have deployed your strategy when I can see it on the shop floor." But I rarely can see it on the shop floor, and I will take my clients, and I will walk to the shop floor and say, "Okay, where is it?" And, "Do these numbers add up to the bottom line figures I saw in your Boardroom?" "How would you know?" "How **quickly** would you know?" It's that linkage that the Balanced Scorecard does not excel at.

Barry Witcher: The BSC [Balanced Scorecard] comes from Hoshin Kanri, but it doesn't use Hoshin as a management of deployment system. In theory, they complement each other. The BSC could be used to formulate and develop corporate-level Hoshins, and Hoshin Kanri used to deploy and manage them in daily management. As one manager told me, the BSC is good at what should be achieved, and Hoshin Kanri is good at how objectives can actually be accomplished. The top is good at telling workers what's got to be done, but not so good at saying how it should be done.

Howard Rohm: Having good performance information delivered to the people who need the information on time and with high business intelligence value is one of the key benefits of a good Balanced Scorecard system. Many scorecards, especially early ones that have not kept up with changes in the underlying concepts of scorecard development, are focused on simple performance measures and data reporting. Modern scorecard systems depend on much more than a software solution for data reporting—they require an understanding of [how] organization strategy, planning, budgeting, alignment, accountability and execution are related. And all this in a climate of change.

There are three main versions of the Balanced Scorecard originally created by Drs. Kaplan and Norton over 20 years ago. The first type—measurement scorecards—are driven by a quest for nonfinancial performance measures to complement the financial measures most organizations currently use. Many early scorecards were built like this and still exist today. It is the original design of the management scorecard; to be successful, organizations need to measure more than financial performance, specifically they need to know about customer satisfaction, internal processes, and the ability of an organization to learn and grow.

The second type is newer and started life five years or so after the first generation. In these scorecards—strategy scorecards—measurement is enhanced by adding strategic measures to operational measures and focusing on strategy execution for competitive advantage. The addition of a strategy map to the original scorecard design provides the basis for this embellishment. Any organization that has kept up with scorecard development improvements would have added or will add strategy mapping to build a more robust system where progress against strategy can be tracked, reported, and acted upon. But, the main focus of these systems was/is still around measurement.

The latest generation of scorecards are truly systems that take previous designs in a new direction. In these systems, the scorecard is used as the basic structure to integrate strategic planning, strategy alignment, and strategy execution into one single system. These systems are built by internal teams, not consultants, who use principles of strategic thinking and change management to develop a holistic system that "connects the dots." The Balanced Scorecard Institute's Nine Steps to Success™ framework, for example, is widely deployed worldwide and was the first framework to incorporate elements of strategic thinking and organization improvement into a single system to help an organization move to higher performance. This framework incorporates change management, leadership development, visioning, goal setting, strategy formulation, risk management, customer value, strategy profiling and mapping, strategic and operational performance measurement development and target setting, initiative priority setting, budget formulation, strategic operational planning, alignment, strategy analysis and execution, and strategy evaluation into one disciplined, easy to understand approach to planning and management. Using this system, employees "get it" and see how the work they do connects to the organizations strategy and goals. Measurement and visual reporting are integral to the framework, but the framework is designed to "change hearts and minds" to get everyone on the same sheet of music.

A modern Balanced Scorecard system not only tells you (everyone in the organization, not just the board, C-level executives, or managers) how your work connects to organization goals, it gives you a roadmap of how to get there, focus on what's important, measure what matters, build accountability for results, and involve everyone in the organization in building a higher performing organization. It does this by aligning the organization around strategy, not performance measures or activities. The process of having employees develop their scorecard system creates accountability and understanding.

A modern Balanced Scorecard system has the following benefits:
- Involves everyone in the organization in the development and implementation of strategy
- Builds individual and collective accountability for results
- Provides a roadmap (through a strategic operating plan) of how to achieve business goals or mission purpose
- Focuses on what's important
- Measures what matters
- Involves everyone in the organization in transforming the organization to a higher performing entity

In our framework, we align "shop floor" actions to enterprise strategy by breaking down high-level strategy into actionable strategic objectives, then cascade the objectives down to business and support units, and then down to employees or teams of employees. Only after objectives are aligned (and ownership for results assigned) are performance measures identified to track strategic progress. This is very different than the approach used in many previous scorecards, which involve a cascading of measures from high-level down to individual activity and project measures. Systems built like this are not strategic; strategic focus gets lost soon if one focuses on measures and projects only. We call people who build scorecards like this "potential new clients!"

HOW ARE HOSHIN KANRI AND LEAN SIX SIGMA RELATED?

Question: *How are Hoshin and Lean Six Sigma related?*

A. Blanton Godfrey: The actions I mentioned earlier can be executed by a task force or via an initiative, and they can also become Lean Six Sigma projects.

John Gaul: Lean Six Sigma problem solvers have impressive skills that should be leveraged to continue transforming the business and provide ongoing solid Daily Management. Most strategy has an element of cost and quality competitiveness, and Lean Six Sigma is the right tool set to apply. In addition, related tools from Design for Lean Six Sigma can lead to breakthrough designs in products, services, and even business models, thereby useful to strategy via Hoshin. Viewing the value-creating activities as a Value Stream (core concept in Lean Six Sigma) at various levels brings proper perspective, scalability, and a better understanding of the impact of the supply chain and the distribution and demand side. I've run into too many green and black belts who are not working on the right things, because their company doesn't really have a strategy, just a bunch of to-dos and projects that are simply improvements to ongoing metrics. There may be initial enthusiasm for their Lean Six Sigma project, but then interest wanes, because the winds of the to-dos have shifted and something else is now more important. This is a waste of talented resources. If a black belt can't get people excited about their project, they are not working on the right stuff—period.

Question: *How do Hoshin Kanri and Lean Six Sigma fit together?*

Beth Cudney: Hoshin Kanri and Lean Six Sigma fit hand-in-hand. Hoshin Kanri provides the strategic goals for the organization. Lean Six Sigma comprises all of the tools necessary to achieve the strategic vision. The continuous improvement projects should be selected based on their linkage to the strategic goals, metrics, and tactics outlined using Hoshin Kanri.

Mark Caponigro: Lean relies on the developing and planning against the big picture view of the company. Focus area and then project selection will be greatly enhanced by a solid Hoshin plan. Closing the loop through Lean efforts we gain a better understanding of the core processes and their respective capabilities. This understanding could/should be used to create the SMART gap and goal setting.

Jonathan Ngin: Hoshin Kanri and Lean Six Sigma fit very nicely together as true Lean Six Sigma implementation focus[es] on developing and respecting people's ability to solve problems and to both run and improve the business via a standardized operating system built on Lean Six Sigma methodology. Hoshin Kanri is about connecting the different levels of the organization and entrusting the right resource is aligned to the "Breakthrough" Strategy. An individual who is trained/exposed to Six Sigma Lean methodology is armed with the right skill set to truly go through the A3 process of Discovery, Analysis, Change, Refinement, and Implementation.

Gary Vance: Hoshin Kanri and Lean Six Sigma fit together well to help us realize our vision. Hoshin Kanri facilitates the clear development and dissemination of our goals, goal achievement plans, and results. Lean Six Sigma principles (waste elimination, respect for the individual, start with the customer, etc.) feed into the Hoshin Kanri planning and Lean Six Sigma tools (kaizen events, DMAIC, 5S, standard work, etc.) enable us to carry out our plans and uncover root problem causes. We need both Hoshin Kanri and Lean Six Sigma to get where we want to go.

Zane Ferry: As need dictates. What I mean is that if you drew a Venn Diagram, with one large circle for Hoshin Kanri and smaller individual circles each representing Six Sigma, Lean, Theory of Constraints, etc., the overlaps and subsets would look different for different organizations. The relationships of those circles would also change over time for an organization [as it] matured and developed different needs. It is not a question of Hoshin Kanri relying on some tools and excluding others. The real question is what needs to be done when and how, by whom, in order for our strategic efforts to succeed and be sustainable over time.

Wes Waldo: When we get down into the deployment aspects, the implementation aspects of Hoshin Kanri, that's when you pull in tools and methodologies like Lean and Six Sigma. Now, people will say that Lean and Six Sigma are more of a philosophy and not a "tool bag," and I get that when you start to think about day in and day out, if you understand that basics principles, it does affect the way you manage. And, actually, I think it makes you appreciate something like Hoshin Kanri. These are not two things that are in competition with one another. I think they're congruent in the way we go about doing things. When I start to look at the lowest level X-Matrix and start to populate action plans, that's where I expect to see things like kaizen events, DMAIC projects, DMADV [define, measure, analyze, design, and verify], Innovation projects, and the like. We should be able to tie the metrics from those events directly back to the metrics we found in our Bowling Chart for Hoshin.

David Thomas: Hoshin Kanri is the "Plan" (Deming/Shewart cycle) part of approach to the implementation of strategy, or in Six Sigma terms the Define, Measure, and Analyze steps. We use Six Sigma to develop and establish our Policy Deployment Matrix (PDM) and, in particular, the Improve and Control steps, to ensure that appropriate resources and skills are available and to deselect activities if appropriate.

With the plan in place, we use Six Sigma again to ensure that each activity in the PDM is successfully analyzed, resourced, implemented, and measured for outputs against key performance indicators and critical success factors. Once the PDM is implemented as a whole, Six Sigma then continues as the process for improvement and achievement of stability within the business.

John Petrolini: One of the most complementary things about Hoshin and Six Sigma is that, if an organization is already "proficient" at Six Sigma, then they should have a sound system of determining and prioritizing the vital few things to improve (which is similar to the process of determining a Hoshin Goal), an administrative system to track and review projects (similar to monitoring progress), and have, hopefully, already instilled a culture of fact-based problem solving. Organizations with a robust Six Sigma program in place significantly increase their probability of successfully implementing Hoshin Kanri.

Barry Witcher: I see the latter (Lean Six Sigma) as a daily management and lower-order dynamic capability. Hoshin is a higher-order dynamic capability; it provides direction for daily management.

Jane Dwyer: Both drive the business and culture change that is needed to achieve the vision and drive the performance expected to reflect that. Hoshin helps to set the destination and direction. Lean process is part of the vehicle that will get you there.

Jim Bossert: Hoshin Kanri and Six Sigma are complementary efforts. Hoshin Kanri depends on good data and projects aligned to it. Six Sigma works on projects that are aligned to the Strategic goals, as well as working on getting meaningful data on process performance. In addition, both are reliant on Voice of the Customer to drive improvement.

Mark McDonald: Hoshin Kanri is how strategy is managed; Lean Six Sigma is one effective means to effect change to support strategic objectives.

David Silverstein: A Lean Six Sigma history certainly should help teach and develop the discipline to use a structured approach like Hoshin. Hoshin is a very structured, methodical approach to the implementation and execution of strategy, so Lean Six Sigma is a good foundation.

No strategy, no strategic plan will be successful if you're not realistic about the fact that you're going to run into obstacles, things that you didn't anticipate—market shifts, customer shifts, competitor shifts—which means you have to be in constant problem-solving mode. To truly execute your Hoshin plan, a good Hoshin plan lays out the very big, bold, metrics-driven objectives where you don't necessarily have all of the answers as to how you're going to achieve those objectives. And, if you don't have all of the answers, then that necessarily says that a big part of executing the Hoshin plan will be problem solving. So, if you do not have a good problem-solving methodology, you are not likely to achieve most of the goals of your Hoshin plan. So, the problem solving is very important.

The third piece is that good Lean and Six Sigma backgrounds and the tool sets and the methodology are a lot about project management. Part of your Hoshin plan is going to be about marketing, part of it is going to be about the financial engineering your company, but a big part of it will be about the operations of your company. If your Hoshin plan does not include elements of continuous process improvement, then I think something is missing from your Hoshin plan. It doesn't need to dominate it. If your strategic plan is *not* about competing on costs and quality, then continuous improvement might be a smaller part of the Hoshin plan. In this day and age, things commoditize very fast, so there are always parts of your business that must be improving in terms of quality, price, and delivery. If that's not in your Hoshin plan, then something is probably missing.

So, Lean and Six Sigma are vital to the upfront discipline required for success with Hoshin, it's vital to the continuous problem solving, and it's also vital to the specific parts of your Hoshin plan that call for continuous improvement.

Steve Darrish: Six Sigma and Hoshin Planning: Both are top-down methodologies that depend on alignment of work/organizations. Both are measurement driven. Putting Hoshin Planning in place helps align organizations to do enterprise-level Six Sigma programmatically. Hoshin Planning can be a readiness exercise for Six Sigma deployments. Hoshin Planning integrates with Six Sigma in that it provides the operating gaps that need to be identified to align the project work with. It ensures that teams/organizations are working on meaningful areas of the business. Hoshin Kanri can be the strategic side of Six Sigma. Without it, organizations are just really doing TQM at some level.

Lois Gold: Think about Lean as an implementation methodology. Remember, the basic premise is about improving, transforming, or creating processes (the strategy, the how), which will enable you to achieve the objective/goal. If you need to drive cost savings, or streamline to create capacity and reallocate resources to other value added work, then Lean is an approach that you can use.

Brian Leonard: Hoshin Kanri, as mentioned previously, is the GPS for a Lean transformation. Without an accurate plan for achieving organizational strategic congruence, Lean initiatives may not be as impactful. Hoshin Kanri lays out the path. Lean tools and our people are the means by which we get there. Hoshin Kanri can be the difference between a successful Lean transformation and a flavor of the month. The Six Sigma methodology, while providing effective concepts for statistical process/quality control, can become a burden if we can't achieve a balance between Lean and Six Sigma. Using the data-driven mindset of Six Sigma to potentially measure the extent of alignment of project work to True North metrics can certainly be an advantage. However, do not allow Six Sigma to slow us to a crawl due to analysis paralysis. This is true not only for Hoshin Kanri, but for Lean in general. Use data to quickly analyze processes and then move forward. Many become so caught up in Six Sigma tools and fail to move forward as quickly as could have been possible. For example, not every data set requires hypothesis testing, but many encounter such pitfalls. Use the data analysis side of Six Sigma to complement Lean, but don't allow it to prevent progress.

James Hinkle: Hoshin Kanri and Lean Six Sigma go perfectly together. Hoshin Kanri allows an organization to focus its efforts in the correct places and timely complete goals and objectives. As this occurs, the amount of time spent on completing the goal is reduced and the benefits of the goal/objective are achieved much sooner. These benefits could include improved safety, quality, delivery, costs, culture, and so much more.

Bob Emiliani: Fits fine with Lean. Does not fit with Lean Six Sigma (wrong time-scale).

Kevin Meyer: I am not a fan of Lean Six Sigma, so I really cannot answer this. I believe that Lean Six Sigma as typically taught and practiced bastardizes two excellent and potentially complementary concepts, thereby leading to a poor and often failed implementation of both/either. Typically Lean Six Sigma includes no recognition/teaching of the underlying philosophy, or especially the critical "respect for people" principle; instead just teaching a subset of tools. Similarly, Lean Six Sigma generally includes just a subset of the Six Sigma body of knowledge. Personal hot button of mine.

INDEX OF EXPERT INTERVIEWS

Michele Bechtell is an international expert in strategic planning and implementation, continual market alignment, and organizational transformation. She has written three books on the subject of Hoshin Kanri including *The Management Compass: Steering the Corporation Using Hoshin Planning* (AMA, 1995).

Lisa Boisvert, principal consultant at Business Centered Learning. Author of *Strategic Planning Using Hoshin Kanri: Implementing Corporate Strategy Through Hoshin Planning* (GOAL/QPC, 2012).

Jim Bossert, PhD, master black belt. Formerly with Bank of America, General Electric, Nokia, Kodak, and Xerox.

Michael Bremer, executive director, Chicagoland Lean Enterprise Consortium and vice president of Association Manufacturing Excellence. Author of several books including *Escape the Improvement Trap* (CRC Press, 2010).

Jim Buchanan, owner at Winning Customer Love, master black belt, formerly with Bank of America.

Mark Caponigro, director, Business Process Transformation at Manpower Group, formerly with Wells Fargo, Bank of America, Honeywell.

Tom Cluley, owner at Above The Fray Advisory Services, LLC. Formerly with The Wiremold Company; author of several books including co-author of *Driving Strategy to Execution Using Lean Six Sigma* (CRC Press, 2012).

Joe Colletti, president of the Woodledge Group. Author of *Hoshin Kanri Memory Jogger* (GOAL/QPC, 2013) and *Focused Planning: Hoshin Kanri–American Style* (Woodledge Group, 1996).

Michael Cowley, PhD, managing partner, CW Consulting Associates, LLC. Formerly with Hewlett-Packard. Co-author of *Beyond Strategic Vision: Effective Corporate Action with Hoshin Planning* (Routledge, 1997).

Beth Cudney, PhD, ASQ Fellow, associate professor, director of the Design Engineering Center, Missouri University of Science and Technology; formerly with Danaher and Dana Corporation. Author of several books, including *Using Hoshin Kanri to Improve the Value Stream* (CRC Press, 2009).

Steve Darrish, director of Lean Enterprise at PricewaterhouseCoopers. Master black belt; formerly with Bank of America and Microsoft.

Mark DeLuzio, CEO Lean Horizons Consulting, LLC. Formerly with Danaher Corporation; helped launch Hoshin Planning while an executive at Danaher.

Paul Docherty, founder and executive director at i-nexus. Developer of "How to Make Hoshin Planning Work: Bridging the Achievement Gap."

Bob Dodge, co-founder of IDI, a management consultancy, former LaMarsh and Associates director of Consulting Services, trusted business advisor, business coach, and peer board facilitator; member of The Alternative Board.

Ellen Domb, PhD, TRIZ consultant at PQR Group. Formerly with GenCorp-Aeorjet. Co-author of *Beyond Strategic Vision: Effective Corporate Action with Hoshin Planning (Routledge, 1997)*.

Jane Dwyer, director of Supply Chain Integration at Knoll. Formerly with Honeywell, GECOM, and Alcoa Fastening Systems.

Bob Emiliani, PhD, principal, The CLBM, LLC; professor at Connecticut State University. Formerly with United Technologies and author of several books on the subject of Lean.

Zane Ferry, Value Stream coach, Ingersoll Rand.

W. John Gaul, Jr., principal consultant, BMGI. Certified Lean Six Sigma master black belt & quality engineer. 20 years manufacturing experience prior to 10 yrs. at BMGI. Contributing writer to: *The Innovator's Toolkit*—Wiley.

A. Blanton Godfrey, PhD, dean at NC State University. Formerly with Juran Institute and AT&T Bell Labs. Author of several books including co-author with Dr. Joseph M. Juran of *Juran's Quality Handbook* (McGraw-Hill, 1999).

Lois Gold, vice president of Enterprise Program Management at MetLife. Formerly with CitiBank and Hewlett-Packard. While director of Corporate Quality at HP, she was involved in translating the original Hoshin Kanri materials for use in the United States.

Jerome Hamilton, vice president, Lean Six Sigma, Corporate Quality & Acquisition Integration (Global) at 3M; formerly with Ford and General Motors.

James Hinkle, director of Operations at Cornerstone; Hoshin planning practitioner.

Tom Jackson, PhD, principal of Rona Consulting Group; author of the Shingo Prize-winning *Hoshin Kanri for the Lean Enterprise* (CRC Press, 2006).

Bob King, co-founder, chairman, and CEO of GOAL/QPC. In the early 1980s, he was the first to launch a regional Deming users group. In the late 1980s, he led the research of advanced Japanese quality methods. He was the first to publish books in English on Quality Function Deployment and Hoshin Planning. He led the adoption of these methods at many U.S. organizations, including Ford, Intel, Procter & Gamble, Hewlett-Packard, IBM, Bethesda.

Rafeek Kottai, president and CEO, founder at Maxxion Technologies Inc. and HoshinOnline.com.

Chandrashekhar Kulkarni, owner, Neptune Engineers.

Jeanenne LaMarsh, executive director of Consulting Services at LaMarsh Global. Developed Managed ChangeT model and methodology and author of many books on change management including *Change Better: Survive—and Thrive—During Change at Work and Throughout Life* (Agate B2, 2010).

Brian Leonard, Lean Six Sigma managing advisor at Purdue Healthcare Advisors.

Jeffrey Liker, PhD, Liker Lean Advisors, professor at University of Michigan. Author of several books, including *The Toyota Way* (McGraw-Hill, 2003).

Mark McDonald, senior Operations Excellence executive; master black belt; formerly with Accenture, George Group, IBM, and Michelin North America.

Mara Melum, president of Minerva Leadership Institute, Inc., Consultant, Executive Coach and author of book, *Breakthrough Leadership: Achieving Organizational Alignment Through Hoshin Planning*.

Kevin Meyer, co-founder and partner of Gemba Academy. Formerly with Abbott Labs; author of several books.

Adrian Mulder, owner of TEAM Lean Six Sigma, The Netherlands. Has performed key roles in various Lean Six Sigma deployments including General Electric, Shell, Caterpillar, Royal Dutch Philips, KLM, ING, and DHL.

Jonathan Ngin, director of Quality and Process Improvement at Express Scripts. Formerly with Honeywell and Tyco.

Judith Oja-Gillam, Business Architecture Practice lead at IAG Consulting. Formerly with Royal Bank of Scotland and HSBC.

John Petrolini, director of Continuous Improvement at Pegasystems. Formerly with Teradyne.

Gerhard Plenert, PhD, president, Institute of World Class Management (IWCM), author of 15+ books including co-author of *Driving Strategy to Execution Using Lean Six Sigma* (CRC Press, 2012).

Howard Rohm, president and CEO of the Balanced Scorecard Institute; author of *The Institute Way: Simplify Strategic Planning and Management with the Balanced Scorecard* (The Institute Press, 2013).

Larry Rubrich, owner, WCM Associates; co-author of *Policy Deployment & Lean Implementation Planning* (WCM Associates, 2009).

Bruce Sheridan, director, Business Transformation, head of Reengineering at Citi Mortgage. Formerly with Bank of America and Florida Power & Light. Master black belt, and author of *Policy Deployment: The TQM Approach to Long-Range Planning* (Quality Press, 1993).

David Silverstein, president and CEO, BMGI. Formerly with Seagate Technology. Author of several books including *The Innovator's Toolkit* (John Wiley & Sons, 2012).

David Thomas, director, D2 Associates (change consultants), Toyota-trained Continuous Improvement specialist. Formerly with Unipart Group of Companies. Co-author of *Build Lean: Transforming Construction Using Lean Thinking* (Ciria, 2011).

Gary Vance, dean of the College of Adult and Professional Studies at Charleston Southern University. Formerly with JW Aluminum, The HON Company, Peterbilt Motors, INA USA, Toyota Motors Manufacturing of Indiana.

Wes Waldo, COO and president of the Americas at BMGI. Formerly with Danaher, Gillette (Duracell), and Ralston Purina (Eveready Battery).

Greg Watson, PhD (ABD), chairman, Business Excellence Solutions, Ltd. Formerly with Hewlett-Packard, Compaq, and Xerox. Author of several books, including *Business Systems Engineering* (John Wiley & Sons, 1994).

Thom Williams, Master black belt, Bank of America.

Barry Witcher, PhD, Reader Emeritus, Norwich Business School, University of East Anglia. Author of several books including co-author of *Strategic Management: Principles and Practice* (Cengage, 2012).

THE CATALYST FOR SUCCESS WITH HOSHIN KANRI

There are a few enablers that will help immensely if you plan to use Hoshin Kanri in your organization. Together, they form the catalyst, the "spark" that will help you ignite the process.

RESPECTFUL and RESPECTED LEADERSHIP

The leadership team is respectful of the employees/associates and the employees/associates truly respect their leaders. I believe that leading with humility aids tremendously in gaining employee/associate respect. Command and control leaders and impactful managers will kill a Hoshin deployment. Look for the leaders with the "What do you think?" versus the "Thou shalt" approach. Move the dictatorial leaders and managers out of the way.

DEMONSTRATED DISCIPLINE

The leadership team and the organization need to have the proven ability to "stick with things" and to "see things through." If this is a problem, do *not* attempt Hoshin.

THE PROVEN ABILITY TO FOCUS

The leadership team and the organization must have proven the ability to "just say no" to initiatives. Selecting the Hoshin objectives is more about deselecting things than it is about selecting new ones. The entire team must be able to select the "critical few" and then resist the temptation to allow the list to expand back to the "trivial many."

A SOLID LEAN FOUNDATION

A foundation built on an understanding of, and application of, the Lean principles is key. The foundation should include extensive experience with Daily Management and the Lean Six Sigma toolset, a Continuous Improvement mindset, and solid project management skills. The aforementioned help provide the discipline the organization will need to be successful with Hoshin Kanri.

A HOSHIN KANRI EXPERT

It helps immensely to have someone on board who has "been there and done that" with regard to a successful Hoshin Kanri launch.

ORGANIZATIONAL CHANGE MANAGEMENT (OCM)

OCM is like "oil for the rusty machinery." It can help you identify and mitigate resistance to: (1) the overall Hoshin Kanri initiative and (2) the improvement projects that will result from the deployment.

With the catalyst in place, enabled by organizational change management, employee engagement starts to grow. The Catchball process helps to increase vertical alignment across the organization. Finally, as more parts of the organization participate actively in the Hoshin process, cross-functional alignment begins to improve. As the Hoshin Kanri process grows in maturity, the business results improve, as represented by the increasing size of the spiral (Figure 3.2).

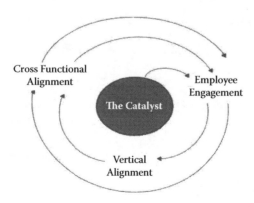

FIGURE 3.2
Hoshin Kanri drives improved business results.

Be the chief but never the lord.

Lao Tzu

Humility is not thinking less of yourself, it's thinking of yourself less.

C. S. Lewis

One of the most sincere forms of respect is actually listening to what another has to say.

Bryant H. McGill

Humility is the solid foundation of all virtues.

Confucius

There is no respect for others without humility in one's self.

Henri Frederic Amiel

Humility is to make a right estimate of one's self.

Charles Spurgeon

Today, no leader can afford to be indifferent to the challenge of engaging employees in the work of creating the future. Engagement may have been optional in the past, but it's pretty much the whole game today.

Gary Hamel

SOME WORDS OF CAUTION

Charles Kettering lived long before the time of Hoshin Kanri, but I believe his words describe it well:

Knowing is not understanding. There is a great difference between knowing and understanding: you can know a lot about something and not really understand it.

Charles Kettering (1876–1958)

… it is often impossible to "think your way into a new way of acting." Rather, guided by correct principles, one may do, observe, learn, and then do something else until we "act our way into a new way of thinking."

John Shook

RECOMMENDED READING

Bechtell, M. 1995. The management compass. New York: AMA Management Briefing.

Cowley, M., and E. Domb. 1997. *Beyond strategic vision: Effective corporate action with Hoshin Planning.* New York: Routledge.

Jackson, T. L. 2006. *Hoshin Kanri for the Lean enterprise.* Boca Raton, FL: CRC Press, Taylor & Francis Group.

Plenert, G., and T. Cluley. 2012. *Driving strategy to execution.* Boca Raton, FL: CRC Press, Taylor & Francis Group.

Sobek, D. K., II, and A. Smalley. 2008. *Understanding A3 thinking: A critical component of Toyota's PDCA management system.* Boca Raton, FL: CRC Press, Taylor & Francis Group.

Appendix A

THE TRADITIONAL WAY

Within an organization that operates in the "traditional way," executives spend their time involved with "strategic matters." Supervisors and operators spend their time on daily activities (i.e., getting the work done). And managers, depending on their role, spend their time working somewhere in between (Figure A.1).

Executives rarely get involved with daily activities unless it's part of a facility tour or an infrequent "all-hands" meeting with employees.

Supervisors and operators rarely get involved in "strategic matters" unless it's listening to the boss explain this year's plan and the flowdown of objectives to their level in the organization.

THE HOSHIN WAY

Within an organization that embraces the "Hoshin Way," people from all levels can play a role in both Strategic and Daily Management. The executives still spend most of their time involved with Strategic Management, but they also might spend some time involved with Daily Management via the Catchball process and review meetings.

The diagram in Figure A.2 shows the time spent on organizational activities. For example, the shaded area represents the time spent on Strategic Management.

Depending on their role, managers might split their time between Strategic and Daily Management.

Supervisors and operators still spend most of their time on Daily Management, but they also might be occasionally involved with strategy deployment and execution via the Catchball process and review meetings.

FIGURE A.1
The Traditional Way.

FIGURE A.2
The Hoshin Way.

Definitions

Strategic Management is about seeing the BIG picture and then guiding the Vision, Values, Mission, and Strategy for the organization.

Daily Management is work carried out that is primarily about shorter-term operational and functional activity. It helps to reduce process variation and daily firefighting, and it creates the organizational stability needed to allow a culture of continuous improvement to thrive.

THE PDCA CYCLE

At the core of Hoshin Kanri is the PDCA cycle, also known as the Deming or Shewhart cycle:

P = Plan   C = Check
D = Do   A = Act (in this book, A stands for "Adjust")

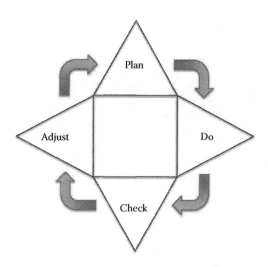

FIGURE A.3
PDCA steps on a five-sided pyramid.

The five-sided pyramid was selected to represent these steps. When you flatten the pyramid, you get (Figure A.3):

Plan = Develop the plan
Do = Execute the plan, take action
Check = Monitor the plan, check the results
Adjust = Make adjustments and make improvements; if the plan is not fulfilled, analyze the cause and take further action by going back to the plan

And once a year, you go through the "Scan" step (Figure A.4):

Scan = Taking steps (explained below) to identify a few key objectives in support of your strategy
Plan = Develop the plan
Do = Execute the plan, take action
Check = Monitor the plan, check the results
Adjust = Make adjustments and make improvements; if the plan is not fulfilled, analyze the cause and take further action by going back to the plan

Scan is about taking some steps to identify a few key objectives in support of your strategy. It presupposes that the organization has done some

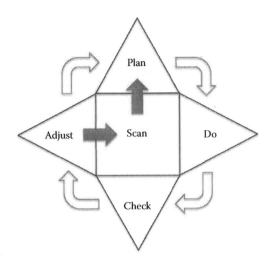

FIGURE A.4
Scan PDCA steps on a five-sided pyramid.

strategy formulation work in the recent past that included an examination of both external and internal influences on strategy to include:

- The external environment
- Industry attractiveness
- Your competitors
- Your value chain
- Your capabilities and competencies
- Your competitive advantage

This step starts with understanding where you are today and where you want to be a few years from now.

The Scan process includes:

1. Develop your Mission Statement
2. Define your Values
3. Define your Current State
4. Define your Vision
5. Design your Desired Future State
6. Identify the Gaps between the Future and Current States
7. Prioritize the Gaps, define your Business Priorities

Appendix B

Note to reader: I know this appears to be hugely complicated, but it's not. For starters, the name itself is a bit of a mouthful, but don't be scared away. The ID is a fairly simple tool, but quite powerful.

INTERRELATIONSHIP DIGRAPH (A.K.A., AN ID, A RELATIONS DIAGRAM)

What Is It?

The Interrelationship Digraph shows cause-and-effect relationships and helps to analyze links between different aspects of a complicated situation.

Why Use It?

- You wish to explore the cause-and-effect relationships among many issues.
- When you have limited resources and need to focus your efforts on one or two priorities.
- You have completed an affinity diagram, fishbone diagram, and you want to more completely explore the relationship of the ideas.

How to Use It?

1. Create a problem statement.

    Example: Jon has too many "gaps" to resolve between his Personal Future State and his Personal Current State and he wants to narrow the list to two or three critical gaps to focus on for closure this year.

2. Assemble a team and agree on the problem/issue.

3. Develop a list of ideas.

    The list can come from a brainstorming session, or from an affinity diagram, fishbone diagram, etc.

4. Record the ideas on separate note cards, pieces of paper, or sticky notes.
5. Lay out the ideas in a circle on the wall and identify each one with a letter or a number (Figure B.1).
6. Ask the team to work together to look for relationships between the items. Start with A. How is A related to B? How is A related to C? How is A related to D? And, so on. Then move on to B. How is B related to C? How is B related to D? How is B related to E? And, so on.
7. If there is a cause-and-effect relationship between two items, draw an arrow from the cause to the effect. If no apparent relationship exists, move on to the next pair of items.
8. Review and revise the arrows until the team reaches consensus regarding the relationships.
9. Now, draw the Interrelationship Diagraph (ID) and tally the Ins and Outs for each item. An In is an arrow pointing toward the item. An Out is an arrow pointing away from the item (Figure B.2).
10. Use the ID information for planning. The items with the most Outs are called Drivers and they are candidates for possible actions to be taken.

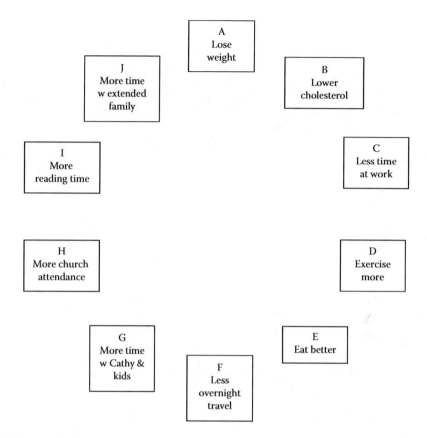

FIGURE B.1
Ideas on sticky notes positioned in a circle form the ID in Chapter 1.

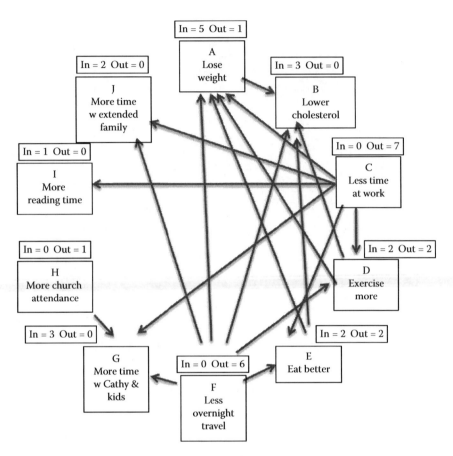

FIGURE B.2
The ID from Chapter 1 with Ins and Outs tallied.

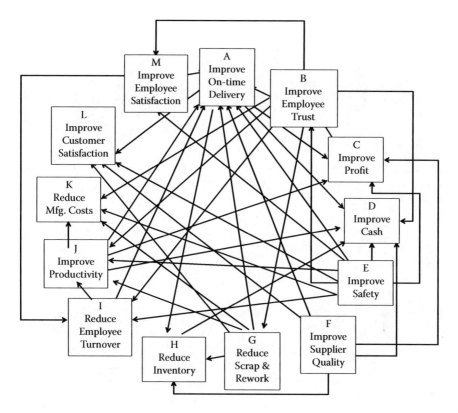

FIGURE B.3
The ID from Chapter 2.

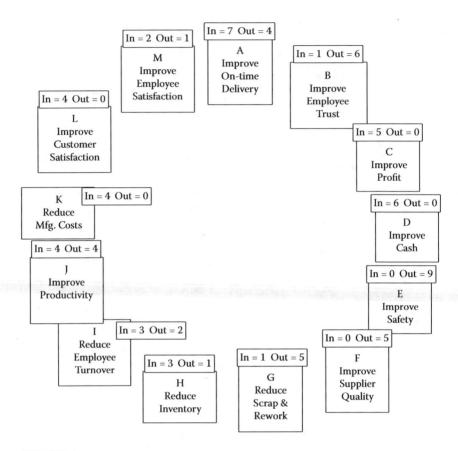

FIGURE B.4
The ID from Chapter 2 with the Ins and Outs tallied.

Appendix C

THE X-MATRIX AND THE A3

What Are They?

"… let's think of Hoshin Kanri in three major steps: 1. Strategy Development; 2. Organizational Alignment; and 3. Execution. The X-Matrix is specifically targeted for Organizational Alignment and the A3 for Execution. Even though they are used at different stages, the X-Matrix and A3 share an attribute. They both serve to provide an organized view of a vast array of information arranged logically to communicate a message or a story that otherwise would be difficult to see."

Bruce Sheridan

Why Are They Needed?

"The X-Matrix links the Long-Term Strategy, Tactical Agenda, Projects, and Metrics all on one page in addition to discussing how the work will be resourced.

The A3 is named for the size of the paper typically used to display the information, A3 or in the US 11" x17". The A3 is used to guide a project team through the execution of their work using predefined steps. During the project, the A3 serves to guide the team through problem solving or lean steps as well as serve as a way to update peers and management on progress. In the end, the A3 serves as a story board documenting the improvement achieved by a project team."

Bruce Sheridan

How Does The X-Matrix Work?

Here's one example (see Figure C.1) of how the X-Matrix is used at three levels in an organization.

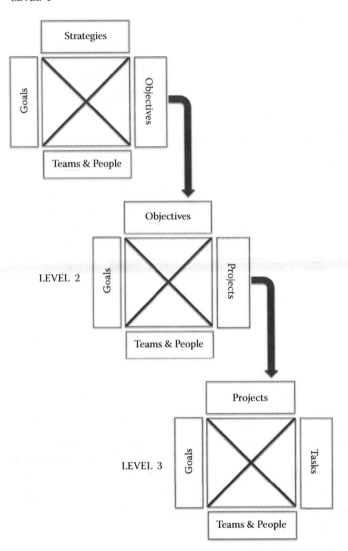

FIGURE C.1
An X-Matrix in use at three levels in an organization.

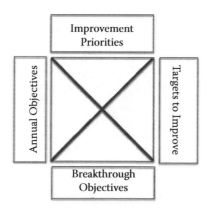

FIGURE C.2
Another X-Matrix example.

At Level 1, the upper level of the organization, Goals (including Hoshins) are included in the X-Matrix, along with Strategies, Objectives, and the Teams and People who will do the work.

At Level 2, the Objectives from the Level 1 X-Matrix replace the Strategies in the X-Matrix's "northern" quadrant and Projects replace Objectives in the X-Matrix's "Eastern" quadrant.

At Level 3, the Projects from the Level 2 X-Matrix replace the Objectives in the X-Matrix's "northern" quadrant and Tasks replace Projects in the X-Matrix's "eastern" quadrant.

Here's another X-Matrix (see Figure C.2) with a different approach to the four quadrants. In this case, we start in the "southern" quadrant of the X-Matrix with Breakthrough Objectives, and then move to the "western" quadrant with the Annual Objectives. The "northern" quadrant includes Improvement Priorities, while the "eastern" quadrant includes the Targets.

More Information About the X-Matrix and A3

See the books on the Recommended Reading list for more information on the X-Matrix and the A3.

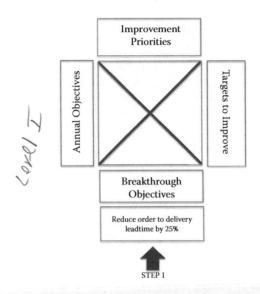

FIGURE C.3
Step 1, Include Breakthrough Objectives (including Hoshins) in the X-Matrix.

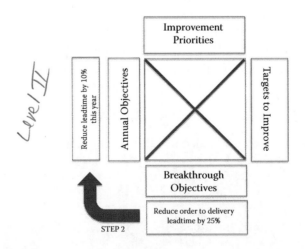

FIGURE C.4
Step 2, Identify Annual Objectives in support of the Breakthrough Objectives.

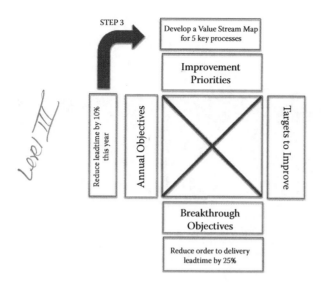

FIGURE C.5
Step 3, Identify Projects in support of the Annual Objectives.

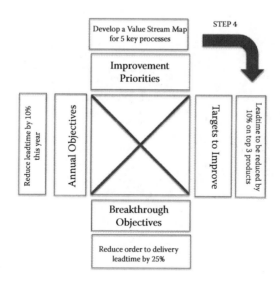

FIGURE C.6
Step 4, Assign Targets to the Projects.

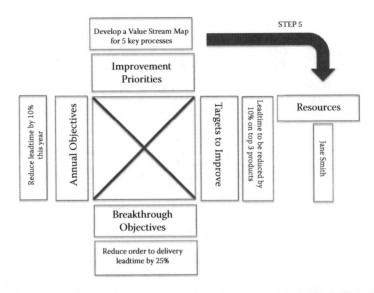

FIGURE C.7
Step 5, Assign Resources to the Projects.

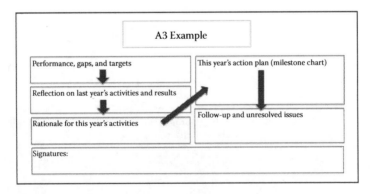

FIGURE C.8
An example of an A3 with steps shown.

Bibliography

Akao, Y., ed. 1988. *Hoshin Kanri: Policy deployment for successful TQM.* New York: Productivity Press, pp. xxi, xxiii. (Printed in English in 1991)

Carroll, L. 2000. *Alice's adventures in wonderland and through the looking glass.* New York/London: Signet Classic Printing/Penguin Group.

Cowley, M., and E. Domb. 1997. *Beyond strategic vision: Effective corporate action with Hoshin Planning.* New York: Routledge, pp. 95, 170–172.

Fayad, V., and L. Rubrich. 2009. *Policy development and Lean implementation planning.* Ft. Wayne, IN: WCM Associates, pp. 88–93.

Jackson, T. L. 2006. *Hoshin Kanri for the Lean enterprise.* Boca Raton, FL: CRC Press, Taylor & Francis Group, pp. 6–9.

King, B. 1989. *Hoshin Planning: The developmental approach.* Salem, NH: GOAL/QPC, pp. 1–10, 1–11.

Sobek, D., and A. Smalley. 2008. *Understanding A3 thinking: A critical component of Toyota's PDCA management system.* Boca Raton, FL: CRC Press, Taylor & Francis Group, pp. x, 11.

Index

About the Author

Randy Kesterson has held executive level positions at General Dynamics and Curtiss-Wright, with prior successful experience at Harsco Corporation, John Deere, and at privately held Young & Franklin/Tactair Fluid Controls.

He also worked as a management consultant to organizations such as Bank of America, Caterpillar, Motorola, Bank of Montreal, Ford Motor Company, Milliken & Company, RJ Reynolds, and the Federal Aviation Administration (FAA).

Randy serves as the Chair of the Advisory Board for the Center for Global Supply Chain and Process Management at the University of South Carolina's Moore School of Business. He earned his Six Sigma Black Belt at North Carolina State University/IES.

He earned his Bachelor of Science Degree in Engineering Operations from Iowa State University and attended Syracuse University where he earned his MBA with a concentration in Operations Management.

Randy and his family live in North Carolina.